NATTY'S POND

Finding hope and forgiveness after a medically advised abortion

A Memoir by

JENNY FOSTER

Natty's Pond: Finding hope and forgiveness after a medically advised abortion
By Jenny Foster

Copyright © 2021 by Jenny Foster

ISBN (Paperback): 978-1-09838-886-7

Unless otherwise noted, scriptures are taken from The Holy Bible, New International Version®, NIV®. Copyright © 1973, 1978, 1984, 2011 by Biblica, Inc.™ Used by permission of Zondervan. All rights reserved worldwide. www.zondervan.com **The "NIV" and "New International Version" are trademarks registered in the United States Patent and Trademark Office by Biblica, Inc.™"**

Cover photo by Jenny Foster

https://www.jennyfoster.org
author@jennyfoster.org

Praise for Natty's Pond

"Memoirs about medically advised abortions are rare. Natty's Pond is also rare in other ways. Because Jenny Foster kept diaries, her memoir contains powerful details, most often forgotten or repressed by those who have experienced trauma. Her heartbreaking abortion story is matched by the uplifting narrative of her complex healing journey. Riveting, sensitive, personal, relatable, unforgettable. An important contribution to our understanding of decisions on abortion and its life-changing impact on women and families."

—Betty McDowell, Vice President, Affiliate Services, Heartbeat International

Natty's Pond is a courageous memoir which everyone should read, whether or not you are suffering from the aftermath of abortion. We all need to be prepared to help those who are believing the lies which motivate abortion. Yes, Jenny Foster's story is difficult but every reader will rejoice in God's powerful work of healing for a hurting woman's life in the midst of grief and pain.

—Kathy Collard Miller, international speaker and award-winning author of over 55 books including *No More Anger: Hope for an Out-of-Control Mom.* **www.KathyCollardMiller.com**

"A heartbeat, then came the news of a son they hoped for and later the diagnosis—words that would cut to the core of her broken heart. Come along as Jenny courageously shares her story of a medically advised abortion and the aftermath that ensued. Through her gift of writing, she pulls the reader into a world she never could have anticipated and join her as she traveled the road called grief. Raw, real and although heartbreaking, her journey also takes her to a place of healing and restoration. Her faith journey is a beautiful display of God's tender mercies, and as her heart and spirit began to heal, she realized her story might help others along their journey. Natty's Pond is riveting and beautifully written. A story of hope and healing and through tragedy, a life redeemed. A must read!"

Jeannie Pittam
Former Post Abortion Services Coordinator
Pregnancy Center, Lincoln NE

"Unless we are willing to venture into the deep, we will build our whole life in the shallows."

Karen A. Ellison, *Healing the Hurt that Won't Heal*

Dedication

For my baby boy, Nathanael, to whom I offer a lifelong opus and a love without end—my angel in heaven. For my husband, Garrett, who stood still in spite of my whirlpools and tidal waves. For my parents, who offered unwavering support. And for Lily, "the spring in my step and the catch in my throat"—my angel on earth.

CONTENTS

CHAPTER 1:

LIFE

(2002)

Still under the influence of anesthesia, I lay with my eyes closed, vaguely aware that opening them would be futile. The pressure of a firm hand on my shoulder brought with it the sudden realization that my legs were paralyzed. I couldn't move. Unable to open my eyes, I became more aware of my body. My feet felt disconnected from my ankles, and what felt like paralysis was a band across my knees lashing me to a hospital gurney. Bright lights intruded like the darts of a migraine through flickering eyelids. I wanted to open my eyes to orient myself, but the pain was searing, and the haze of lingering medication felt safer than what I feared awaited me in the recovery room. The jarring thud of wheel locks beneath me signaled that the gurney had stopped moving, and I hesitantly peeked through wet eyelashes in a panic to place myself. Two nurses hovered above me like pastel angels, hooking up oxygen and reassuring me that it was okay to cry. The clock on the wall said 12:10, but it was like trying to read through pool water. Feeling embarrassed, I pushed through the fog of anesthesia enough to apologize to the nurse at my left shoulder who was dabbing at her own eyes with the back of her blue-gloved forearm. The words came from my mouth before my mind could catch them.

1

"I'm so sorry. I'm sorry. I hope I wasn't the one who was screaming?"
Gaining lucidity by the minute, I struggled to lift my head from the pillow
wedged awkwardly behind me on the black vinyl bed.

"Let's have you sit up a bit. Slowly now."

I blinked away the sting of salty tears. I could see the clock clearly now
and it read 12:15. My eyes frantically scanned the recovery room full of
empty beds to find something with which to center myself. As the nurses
adjusted the pillow it hit me, and it hit hard. It was my own voice that had
been screaming as I climbed out of the murky weight of unconsciousness.
My brain caught up to my body like a roller coaster coming to a stop, then
it began again, a guttural, almost primal groaning turned into sobs. The
increasing intensity of the pain made it real—so palpably real—and I
was more present than I wanted to be. There was no way to jump up and
run out of this, so I tried to catch my breath between sobs and gulps until
I was distracted by the familiar burn in my wrist. A cold and tiny finger
traced up my arm, to my neck, and there it was—the metallic chill of IV
medication at the back of my throat. I could see the nurse on my left who
had long, dark hair. She had given me Valium, and I welcomed the heaviness
as it came over me and my head began to separate from my body. I knew
the drug wouldn't last long, but for another twenty minutes, a good kind
of numbness was my comfort. My baby was gone.

ᔕ Journal entry (June 2000)

I plugged the brown hairdryer into the outlet closest to the end of her pastel-quilted bed, as she half leapt, half crawled up to join me with two books precariously clenched in her pink and fleshy hands. It was my favorite time of day, the hour after bath which marked the arrival of our nightly ritual of reading to connect with each other and wind down. During book time, my phone was deliberately left in my bedroom on silent. This was intentional, a time in which to be wholly present and to focus, to forget about everything on my task list and to just be. One-on-one time to be a mom reading to her little girl in a safe and snuggly spot—our little family of two.

"You got your books ready?" I got up on my knees to reposition myself behind her, hairbrush and blow dryer in hand. She placed the books in front of her bare feet, deliberately but gently.

"Mama, I wanna read this one first and then this one." She directed me to look at how she had laid the books out on the bed.

"Oh, that sounds like a great plan. You love *The Velveteen Rabbit*. How do you spell 'rabbit'?"

She stuck her tongue out to the side as she leaned down to put her eye within an inch of the title, as if that would help her sound it out.

"R-A-B-B-I-T?"

"That's right." She sat up in order to scooch backward into the warm rhythm of the hair dryer.

We had washed her huge mane of hair every other night since her first night in the hospital after she was born, and the process of drying her thick and puffy hair was ritualized for us both. I turned off the dryer just long enough to gather a disheveled mop of locks into a plastic clip at the top of her head. Her hair was so dense I had to dry it in three sections. I switched the hair dryer back to the warm setting and closed my eyes for a minute, taking in the familiar damp and clean smell of her hair mixed with tea tree and cucumber tearless shampoo. It was my favorite smell—not just any clean hair and soap smell, but the way it mingled with the comfort found in clean pajamas and crisp sheets. I felt immediately calmed by it.

"Ouch! Mama, stop!" She screeched as I gently pulled the brush through her hair, coated with detangling spray.

"I'm sorry, bunny, but if I don't brush it you know it'll turn into a rat's nest in the back."

"Okay, silly face," she teased, and I returned the gesture by tickling her exposed foot.

She shrieked with delight, and I dropped the hair dryer on the bed and wrestled her down and then slid her up toward the pillows. She reached up to her headboard to feel around for her beloved blanket, and in a flash, she threw it across her forehead and stuck her thumb in her mouth. I pulled her feet up in the air and tucked them under the sheets, having to complete this ritual twice to get clean socks on my blanket-blindfolded toddler. I took my nightly position on her left, against the wall where there wasn't much room for me amidst her large sorority of stuffed animals. We cozied up together to share the pillows, and she liked it when we held the book together with my arm over her so I could see the pictures from her point of view. She wasn't old enough to be reading tonight's selection of books, so I began the story in the most animated narrator voice I could muster.

She giggled as if it was the first time she'd heard the opening line of the book, though we'd read this one at least two dozen times.

"Look what the bunny is doing. Silly bunny!" We both laughed, and as I turned the page, I asked her to find the horse in the next scene. I was so comfortable in her cozy bed after a long day that I nearly dropped the book on us when I dozed off.

"Mama! KEEP reading." I readjusted my shoulders around her and pressed on with the most outrageous and funny voices I could pull from my repertoire, and I marveled at how she belly laughed, as if she hung on my every word.

"Okay, we finished our two books, so it's time to go to sleep." Unlike many four-year-old little people, she didn't protest but clenched her blanket tighter and found her thumb again. I pulled her closer to me, and the fresh smell of her clean hair gave me a feeling reminiscent of when she was an infant. I doubted if there was a place closer to heaven than these moments with her. I smoothed her hair into place and pulled the quilt higher onto her shoulder. The familiar sound of a wet thumb popped out of her mouth.

"Night-night, Mama," she mumbled through her loose-knit blanket.

"Mama?"

"Yes, bug."

"Can I work in the same office where you work?"

"Well, that's a good question." I stalled trying to think of what would be age appropriate.

"I think that first you have to keep reading every night, and go to school, and eat your carrots like the little rabbit in the book, to grow up strong. One day you'll know where you want to work, but you don't have to know right now." I was quiet to see what my precocious and pensive toddler planned to throw at me next.

"I already know where I want to work. I want a desk right next to your desk so I can see you every day and we can still read every night."

"That sounds really nice. I like your plan. Why don't we keep that in our minds and see what happens when you grow up?"

"Mama?" I was getting sleepy and my eyes were closed, though I was listening intently.

"Yes, baby."

"Will you stay here until I fall asleep?"

"Yes, I will."

"Promise?"

"I promise."

The light of the long summer day began to change, and it cast a pink hue over her room, as the sun started to set across the bay. In that light, her hair always looked gold, and her cheeks were getting pink with the coming warmth of sleep.

"Night-night, bunny."

"I love you, Mama," she mumbled with her thumb half out.

As I listened to her rhythmic breath shift into the silence of sleep, I kissed the back of her head and extricated myself from her twin bed, with stealth, so as not to wake her. I lingered in her doorway to take in the last remnants of babyhood that still showed themselves when she slept.

"I love you, too."

CHAPTER 2:

INNOCENCE LOST

(1984)

There was a particular toy I kept carefully put away in the corner of the tall, white, over-the-desk bookshelf in my childhood bedroom. I waited a long time to get it. I was embarrassed that I liked baby dolls until the end of my twelfth year, and I didn't get the memo that playing with dolls wasn't cool until it was a little too late. I was in seventh grade—junior high, middle school, and almost a teenager. Though age-appropriately self-conscious about other things, like what I wore or the style of my hair, I didn't care about being teased by a few friends on occasion for this. I had seen the piles of stuffed animals and a few dolls in the closets of their more mature bedrooms. My love of playing with dolls, at least in the privacy of my room, still outweighed the fear of losing my status as a popular kid.

It wasn't until I was much older that I realized my love for dolls had everything to do with being an only child. I liked stuffed animals and 1980s classics like Rubik's Cubes and multi-colored Slinkies too, but I only liked dolls that looked realistic, the kind you could diaper and pretend were real babies. I never wanted a collectible doll in a box or Barbies who were not easily wrapped in a blanket and fed a life-sized bottle. When I was young, my dolls were often an imaginary baby brother or sister. I didn't have a sibling of my own, so I had to improvise.

I attended Catholic school in the 1970s and 80s, which at that time meant that all of my friends but one came from large families. Until I was old enough to figure out a few things, I was confused about why I was the only kid in my family. In my house you could hear a pin drop on any day at any time, and I spent every possible opportunity at my friends' houses, loving the intimate chaos found around their dinner tables. There were food fights and other disputes that broke out between siblings. If I wasn't at Meegan's, Ellie's, Susan's, Beth's, or Maggie's house, my ever-patient mom was hosting a slumber party at our house with enough girls to form a basketball team.

My favorite toy with its place of honor at the top of my shelf, I'm ashamed to say, was a Cabbage Patch Kid. The coveted and costly doll of the 1980s led many desperate parents to wait in long lines at Christmas, entering bidding wars to lay claim to a Cabbage Patch doll for their child. Purported to be "one of a kind," named, registered, and certified, mine came with a bald head that smelled like baby powder. My friend Maggie got hers at the same time, and we played with them in spite of the coming shadow of puberty. For me, the hidden hallmark of being a "tweener" was wildly incongruent, made up of equal time spent with doll babies and chasing boys.

In 1984 I needed a stern older sister to counsel the self-conscious twelve-year-old me— someone to tell me to go to my room and play earnestly with the toys of my childhood, because boys could definitely wait a few years. I doubt it would have worked, because being one of the popular girls came with an extra layer of social opportunities. I felt unspoken pressure to be part of the trendsetting pack, and the attention of a certain boy who was the school ringleader lured me from the safety of my childhood room. It wasn't long before my Cabbage Patch Kid—the last of my dolls—was relegated to the top shelf of my closet, and the quest for blue eye shadow and pink hair gel eagerly began.

I was sure the butterflies in my stomach meant that I really liked our class leader, Chet, and there was a daily tidal wave of giggling support from my girlfriends to accept this boy's every invitation. On the dodgeball field at recess, he sat by me any chance he could get, and he let me cut in line on Thursday hot dog days. In class he passed me intricately folded notes through mutual friends, and before I knew it, Chet and his posse of pimple-faced teen boys were walking me home from school.

One Saturday, my friends were over at my house in the late afternoon for a slumber party when we heard a clicking sound at my bedroom window. Meegan peeked out from behind the crisp, white JCPenney's curtains to see him pop up from behind the pink camellia bushes. Chet furiously motioned to her to open the window. He was terrified my dad would spot him nosing around the house. Meegan cracked the window and whispered, "You've gotta get out of here!"

His sales pitch back to her was something like, "Her dad won't notice if the rest of you stay here."

Meegan quietly slid the aluminum window closed on its track but wasn't quiet about exclaiming, "He wants you to go for a walk with him!"

Hysterics began amidst my gaggle of girls as they leapt to my dresser to turn on my curling iron and locate my oversized red can of aerosol hair spray. I was so nervous I kept blinking as Beth tried to put mascara on me, leaving something that resembled a Rorschach ink blot smeared across my nose. We snuck downstairs to the basement laundry room and acted like we were on an innocent mission to hang out in the backyard. Within minutes, Ellie had formed a plan, and I was slipping out the back gate by the giant pine tree.

The journey up the street and around the corner felt like one of the longest walks of my life. I hoped I'd correctly understood Meegan's instructions about where to meet Chet. I was excited but dreading our meeting at the same time. I wished my parents were out of town, and I was terrified that an acquaintance would wave to me or, worse yet, a nosy neighbor might call my parents if they saw me with a boy. Head down, I watched the sidewalk closely, afraid to accidentally trip, because if Chet saw me stumble, I was sure I'd have to move to another city. I heard the sound of rubber on concrete, and I looked up to see him sliding to a stop on his BMX bike behind a large hedge in the driveway just ahead of me. I was unimpressed by his rubber-burning performance. I walked a little slower to the driveway to find him propping up his bike between an unknown neighbor's garage door and a brick planter. Loitering in someone's driveway seemed a completely normal place for two awkward kids to navigate their first solo conversation.

I tried to act cool, but my stomach betrayed me with wriggling knots that felt more like bats than butterflies. We didn't talk about anything of substance, and I felt lightheaded from the smell of his Pert Plus shampoo, sweat, and Colgate toothpaste. We stalled awkwardly for a few minutes, but I told him I had to get back or my dad would kill me. Chet quickly put his arm over my shoulder and with the finesse of a much older boy, he kissed me quick and hard on the lips. I knew what to do because I'd studied the kissing scenes in teen movies with keen focus. I heard a car door slam, but before I could push him away in fear of being found out, there was a tongue in my mouth. I pulled away involuntarily and said I had to go. I heard his bike pedals catch a gear, but I didn't look back. The walk home was much faster because I was practically running. I felt like I was going to be sick. I willed myself not to swallow because I was so grossed out thinking that his saliva was in my mouth. I wanted nothing more than to get to the seclusion of the house and brush my teeth.

I could see Beth up ahead, peeking out the front door of my house to see if I was coming down the street yet, and when she saw me, three other inquiring faces joined her. I ran up the front walkway, and thankfully they quickly folded my wobbly-kneed form into the house.

"I can't talk. I HAVE to brush my teeth! I'm so grossed out."

Seventh grade began with all the imaginable adrenalin and antiperspirant befitting a pre-teen parade. If there was any chance that our gaggle of girls could see Chet and his clan of followers, we took it. Puberty arrived in full swing that year for all of us, and by now my friends had crushes on some of the other boys, but their relationships had not yet progressed to kissing. Unfortunately, my friendship and other confusing feelings for Chet grew, and that first nauseating kiss progressed to full-scale making out over the next month of after-school walks and secret encounters.

By the fall of 8 grade, we weren't just kissing in the back row of movie theatres; we were making it just about all the way around the bases every time we saw each other. Things continued heating up, and because his parents both worked, we had far too much unsupervised time. Close to my fourteenth birthday, Chet kept saying, "I know what we should do for your birthday." Whenever he'd bring up sex in a roundabout way, I felt equally terrified and excited. Few of my friends had done anything much but an awkward peck or handholding with their crushes, which seemed about the right speed, but he and I were somehow the unspoken leaders of the junior high sexuality movement. I didn't question how far ahead we were of others because we were certain we were in love. So many things about our time together at school, walking home, going to school dances, setting new trends in our class, and the creative love letters he wrote with intricate cartoons and sketches made me feel important, visible, and loved.

Chet spent weeks planning it out, and I just floated along with the excitement of it all. Barely fifteen himself, he had already done this with another girl two years prior. His skills at kissing and other smooth moves made it clear that he'd definitely had some hands-on experience. I was tightly wrapped up in what I thought was love, and my favorite movies illustrated the loss of innocence tenderly, making me want what they appeared to have. I was unaware that the couples in the movies didn't actually have sex, and they also had the benefit of studio lighting, special effects, and airbrushing, mixed with a tender and professionally produced soundtrack. I thought it was romantic that he'd seen to all the details of his parents being away from home and setting up a kind of nest for us equipped with a blanket, flashlights, and a Radio Shack cassette player. Awkward and innocent, one of the most precious things I had to give away to a boy was lost in the dark and dirty crawl space under his dad's workshop.

I want so much to go back in time to talk to fourteen-year-old me, to wrap her up in a giant quilt of motherly wisdom and ask her, "Why did you value yourself so little to give up your innocence at that age…in that place?" The experience of that afternoon was in no way abusive, and Chet was not a bad guy. My world was about to expand to a much larger campus of high school halls and a bevy of boys who seemed more mature than those from my small private school. My first junior high love with Chet lasted almost two years and set me up for a continued pattern of serial sexual monogamy with a tangled mess of messages that spoke worthlessness over my body.

At a fabric store, you can buy double-faced ribbon that boasts two "right" sides that are identical in pattern and sheen, and both sides look good from any angle. In other words, there is no wrong side, no rough side. Less expensive ribbon has a back side that is meant to be hidden and neatly tucked away when tying bows on pretty packages. My tiny family of three could be found looking outwardly presentable and downright perfect on one side, but the "back" side of our fabric looked and felt quite different. No family is perfect, and we were no exception. We cleaned up good. Within the tight-knit community of a small, private school, it was important to make sure your ankle socks weren't inside-out and that you wore the right name-brand sweater. When our front door was closed and the garage door hit a mechanical stop from the Sears Genie automatic garage door opener, the chemistry often changed in our house, especially by the evening. Life at home floated under and around my dad's moods and compulsions like San Francisco fog. When he wasn't home, I could breathe. If his loud, vintage work van pulled up to the house, a hard fist of anxiety squeezed my sternum in cadence with the sound of his work boots on the stairs. It wasn't until midway through high school that I began to realize that what my guidance counselor called "walking on eggshells" was not the norm in all families. I was a jumpy kid, an intense child, focused on perfectionism and performance, because I thought that if I was better than just good enough, things would stay balanced at home for longer stretches of time. I had swallowed the fishhook with the bait, thinking I had some control over the adults in my life. As I got older, these patterns of tension and hyper-vigilance became hardwired into my nervous system, and without another sibling with whom to share this responsibility, by college I lived in a state of floating baseline anxiety.

We were not a practicing Christian family, but when I was fifteen my dad became deeply involved with a legalistic church that nearly split up my nuclear and extended family. My parents and I experienced deep spiritual wounding during these years of rule-laden Christianity, landing me squarely in a season far away from God. I felt I was getting more than a daily multivitamin of the Bible at Catholic school, and I had no lingering appetite for any supplemental or conflicting religious instruction from my dad. Mom and I reluctantly attended a handful of services and social events at his church, where I sensed tension and an unfamiliar social awkwardness in some of the other teenagers and college students. There was a feeling that came over me around the pastor of my dad's church that triggered the anxious knot that lived in my stomach. Something was off that I didn't care to investigate, and I was a busy high schooler focused on school, friends, and a serious boyfriend. My dad's need to find God at that time in his life was admirable, and I respected him for ultimately leaving that church. He later asked me to forgive him for the pain poured out over our family by his affiliation with this limiting and legalistic church, and I did forgive him. If only forgiveness came with a magic eraser that could wipe away the blurred confusion of my high school and college memories surrounding religion and sex. I needed pruning shears sharp enough to cut and untangle the barbed wiring of my changed childhood brain.

CHAPTER 3:

UNWORTHINESS

(The 80s)

Ifelt a fingernail, as sharp as pruning shears, poking at me hard above my left shoulder, and I immediately whipped my head around at attention. There she was—the nun who only came to our school campus to partake of mass on holy days or for fancy meetings in larger rooms of the church rectory. I had never been introduced to her, but when she appeared out of nowhere, I'd scan her for details. Her face was tense and drawn and reminded me of a shrunken apple doll I made at church camp. She was painfully thin, and her glasses with plain metal rims were too small for her face—simple, just like her grey wool A-line skirt and thin charcoal cardigan. She wore black leather lace-ups with wavy gum soles, rendering her movement about the church campus covert and silent. She'd never come this close to me before, and I was utterly terrified to look up at her. I was taught to make eye contact with adults, but at school it was to be done fleetingly, reverently, sheepishly, which had served me well and kept me out of trouble. She poked me again, this time with more impatient intention, so I looked up—finally my chance to figure out what color hair she had under the black fabric veil that covered her head like a ladies' slip, secured with a coif.

"Tsss. Zip zip. Come with me and be quiet about it." She had already turned on her gum shoes, leaving me where I sat in the church pew. Grabbing my navy cardigan, I caught up to her without a sound.

I knew it would be wrong to ask any questions. I followed like an imprinted chickadee, weaving left and right across the lot of parked cars. At the rectory garden, she took a footpath around the side of the building to a door I had never noticed on my occasional illegal Nancy Drew explorations. She unlocked the side entrance with a key attached to a simple blue rubber band on her wrist, and when she opened the door a rush of fragrance hit me hard. The smell was a kaleidoscope of plain candles, stale water, and men's cologne. I was only nine, and I was frightened by her silence. Other adults who came to get us from our classrooms for various reasons talked to us along the way and usually told us where we were going. She showed me to a tiny room with a 1960s green felt couch, a single hardwood chair, and a small kneeling bench in front of a crucifix with three candles and an open box of matches. She lighted effortlessly on the hard chair but didn't ask me to sit down on the couch, so I remained standing, thinking it was the only thing to do.

"Well, take a seat. What are you waiting for?"

I sat without sitting, a skill I had already mastered. I knew how to sit without letting my bones settle in, ready to run at a moment's notice.

"Yes, ma'am." I nearly choked because that was wrong. She was a nun, a sister. *I should have called her sister,* I worried, but I didn't know her name.

"Zip zip! We won't be here long, but it has come to my attention that you are participating in some of the sacred sacraments along with your schoolmates."

I frantically scanned my mind, trying to think of each time I had gone up to receive communion, relying on my friends to be loyal with their silence. As one of only two non-Catholic families in the parish, I suddenly realized I was caught, was likely going to hell, and the coals of hellfire were being stoked in another room full of melting candles.

"What do you have to say for yourself, then?"

I crossed my ankles and cleared my throat, searching for the meekest voice I could try on. "I'm sorry. I did go up to take communion at Easter mass."

"Communion?" she cut me off and a patch of red came across the small area of her neck that was visible.

"Yes, ma'am. I mean, Sister. I'm sorry." I looked down at my lap, taking hold of a large royal blue button, grasping for anything that might keep my head from floating away.

"I called you in here to make it very clear to you today that you are never again to enter the priest's chambers for confession."

"Oh, that. I'm so sorry. I didn't understand."

"Well, you can take your apology up with the Lord by the intercession of a priest if you become Catholic one day, but I'm not here to take your confession. You are never to receive the Holy Sacrament of Reconciliation again. I know that a certain teacher you had in second grade, who I will remind you is no longer here, may have looked the other way when you participated with the other children. I will give you the benefit of the doubt that somehow in spite of all the education you have received at the graciousness of this institution, you did not fully understand the order of the receipt of the sacraments."

"Thank you, Sister. I understand."

"Your parents pay tuition for you to attend this fine school, and they pay a pretty penny for it. But just because you are a student here, does not mean you are a member of this parish. What I am saying means something, and for you it means that you cannot and will not participate in any portion of mass other than to stand and sit and kneel at the appointed times. You are no longer allowed to participate in Holy Communion here. When your fellow pupils go to line up to receive the Eucharist, you are to stay seated in the pew."

I was too frightened and confused to understand the magnitude of her warning, but her words spoken that day ushered in a new era of what I had yet to understand was shame in my life. I stood up, feeling unworthy to sit on her green couch.

"Do I make myself clear?"

"Yes, ma'am. I mean, Sister. I'm sorry."

"Stop apologizing and just do the right thing from this day forward. You are not Catholic, and unless you or your family become Catholic, you are never again to make a mockery of any of the holy sacraments." She scanned me from my shoes up.

"Your uniform blouse is untucked along the back. Fix it before we return to the church."

I tucked it in quickly and discreetly, and I put on my blue uniform sweater not only as an act of compliance, but also to feel safer, covered. It felt better than having bare arms in this room. I sniffed to keep my nose from running.

"I'll get you a tissue so you can blow your nose."

I felt off balance wondering if she meant to be kind.

I slipped into the end of the pew in the last line of my classmates, never looking back to see if she was gone. I belonged in the second row with the other *Ds* in the alphabet, but the humiliation of being noticed was unbearable. I pulled my skirt down to the top of my knee socks, wishing it was longer, and I tucked my hair behind my ears, placing my hands reverently on my lap. It was automatic for me to hold my hands in the shape of a cup, ready to receive the holy host, but my cup would remain empty for more than a decade.

I was thankful to have a complexion that never showed if I was blushing or flustered. Did my classmates know what had happened? I had already been living on the outside looking in, but I knew I'd have to take my job of fitting in at school to a whole new level. I loved spelling bees, and I thought of the spelling word Peter had missed the week before—*modus operandi*. Catholic school had taught me many good things, and some bad things, but it was often useful to have a modest command of Latin. My *modus operandi* changed forever that day. Even at nine, I knew something about my meeting with Sister was wrong, but I didn't know how to put words to it. I would work hard to remain popular without overstepping the invisible lines that "Sister Zip Zip" had clearly painted in the chalk outline around my pagan body. I would learn to be seen without being seen. I would learn how to matter to someone, to anyone, no matter how dangerous they might be.

This tension in my childhood set an early backdrop for shame and unworthiness, and it was the scaffold onto which I piled the building blocks of my religious education. At times, I felt like I was in a pressure cooker on all sides, and my only escape was a silent and unnoticeable rebellion found in a steamy wisp of secret sexuality.

It became easier in high school to blend in. I was a cheerful and funny girl, but underneath was a storm of compliant perfectionism, a high need for intimacy in whatever form I could get it, and a self-regulating pardon of "anything is okay if I don't get caught." It was a trifecta of trouble. I was certainly not the first girl "looking for love in all the wrong places," but I was conditioned to accept relationships that someone with a higher sense of self-esteem and a stronger moral compass might have avoided.

As an only child, I was lucky to have the exclusive love of my parents and the benefit of the finest education and resources available in a large city in the Bay Area. By high school graduation, as the developmental task of separating from my parents arrived, I felt like a racehorse ready to be released from the starting gate, running from the heavy reins of enmeshment that I later learned are common in single-child households. I left my home accustomed to an angry dad, which made angry boyfriends feel like a familiar set of pajamas.

My high school boyfriend and I both believed that we would go to hell if we had sex before marriage. He was raised in a Christian family actively practicing their faith, and my religious and sex education stoked the flames of eternal damnation we agreed were waiting for us if we kept giving in to our fleshly desires. The edict of damnation, however, only applied to sexual intercourse. There were loopholes, and we took all of them.

We may not have done family life in a functional Christian setting until I was grown and living on my own, but I was definitely taught core values of integrity, work ethic, and the Golden Rule. My family discussed problems going on in the world or tough situations that friends were facing from a practical perspective. The correct answer seemed obvious, because you always did what was right, and took the high road. There wasn't a need for prolonged discussion because there was only one way.

My mom was a well-educated and trained professional in social work with a vast medical vocabulary. She was easy to look up to, and though she could be submissive at times, she came into her own in her mid-30s and 40s. What she didn't say in words, she communicated with her presence. I was watching my parents grow up just as they were watching me grow up. In the backdrop of the 1970s and early1980s, I saw my mom evolve from fearful to fierce in her career during a time when women were standing up in the business world and expanding their influence. I got the message loud and clear that advanced education was not up for discussion, that I would be going to college, and that I could be anything I wanted to be. My parents didn't come out directly and tell me they were pro-choice. My dad was silent on the issue, and it was an unspoken assumption from my mom that women had the right to choose, especially in situations of rape, incest, or if the mother's life was in jeopardy. Most conversations relating to sex or the body were managed with silence.

Overnight, I left the silent echo of an only-child home to join five college roommates in a university-owned apartment. Not only was it nearly impossible to sleep in my new surroundings with noise around the clock, but

I was at ground zero of a collegiate sex marathon. Though I didn't head off to college as an innocent virgin, I was still naive in many ways. The stage was set for me to be physically ready to engage in sexual relationships, whether or not I was emotionally prepared for the natural consequences. College was a sharp contrast to the underground and taboo sexuality of my Catholic school life.

The physical desire for a regular sexual relationship was fueled around me on all sides by my peers, providing the kindling and the lighter fluid for my decision to jump into full sexual intimacy with my first college boyfriend. Faced with the topics of sex and abortion in the first quarter of my freshman year of college, I didn't look to my family roots to find an obvious true north on these issues. There wasn't an anchor to hook onto for these secret topics, so as far as sex was concerned, I went with what felt good for my body as long as I practiced obsessive paranoia about birth control. The intensity of sex was beginning to impact my life, and an indelible mark was left on my heart by the abortion experience of two of my roommates. I hold vivid images of these fractured girls coming home from the procedure and going off to their bedrooms to cry and rest. I was silently supportive, compassionate, and ready to help if they needed anything. My roommates were quiet about it, and I made the assumption that either it faded away or they filed it away. Both of these abortion experiences with friends happened before I was twenty, and in neither case did we discuss the details of what happened, nor did I hear debate about any option other than abortion. At that time in my life, I didn't think about other options, and I certainly didn't question what they were doing. I held no secret judgment about their decisions, and I was incapable of holding a strong position on abortion. I was deeply respectful of private matters, and I didn't think it was my place to judge them. I only knew it was my place to be their friend. Their decisions to have abortions made sense to me based on assumptions I grew up hearing. "She's too young to have a baby." "She's come too far to drop out of school." "She can't afford to have a kid." These statements seemed like completely logical reasons to end a pregnancy. If something made sense rationally, that was the primary filter through which I made my decisions. I had yet to meet God in an intimate way, and Jesus was still up on the cross bleeding, so I wasn't sure how He was going to help.

CHAPTER 4:

HEIRLOOMS

(2020)

There's an old clock on the wall in our home that counts the seconds loudly like a metronome. Its intrusive tick-tock is as comforting as it is distracting. I often position myself near it to do quiet work when I'm alone in the house. My past is memorialized in this family heirloom and other antiques, old photos, and treasures like my grandma's aluminum lemonade spoon from the 1940s. I've carefully preserved needlepoint samplers and pillows made by my grandmother and aunts because they bring me joyful memories—flashbacks that are simultaneously dusty and vivid. I'm protective of furniture that has been passed down to me, and I keep mementos of my daughter's childhood in sealed bags in waterproof totes. My love of family heirlooms stems from a deep desire to feel connected to family, to people, to something.

Every Sunday my husband, Garrett, whom I married in 2008, winds the old clock before the rhythm of its heartbeat begins to extinguish, and wherever I am in the house, I can hear the warm sliding sound the wooden drawer of the clock makes when he opens it for the key to wind it. It's the same sound I heard all the times I saw my grandfather, "Pop Pop," climb up onto the mammoth brick hearth in their home to wind the clock. I can hardly bring myself to open the clock drawer, because after all these years the lingering smell of stale smoke infused with wood takes me back to their elegantly appointed home in an instant. If I close my eyes and let it transport me there, I hear football commentators passionately debating a touchdown on Pop's old Zenith TV. The speakers on either side of the giant mahogany television are larger than the screen itself, covered with pleated gold and glitter-infused fabric. I feel the cold of the marble table against the outside of my arm, as I wait my turn at the bowl of sour cream and onion dip. Someone next to me opens a Coca-Cola and pours it over ice, and I can feel the blue shag carpet under the palm of my hand, as I sit propping myself up on the floor around that table. My cousin rustles through the See's candies looking for her favorite flavor on the bottom layer of a two-pound box. The mothers talk in fast circles in the kitchen as they busily multitask to pull all the courses for dinner together at the same time. Onion and garlic-infused steam rolls out of the kitchen, dissipating in the dining room before it reaches my nose. The floor upstairs squeaks as my grandfather goes up to get a leaf for the dining room table from the closet, and if I listen closely, I can separate the unique timbre of each of their voices, voices of my past. I close the clock drawer and in an instant they're gone.

The story of what led up to Natty's Pond and the aftermath that followed forever changed me. I hold tightly to the heirlooms of my life because they seem unchanging. They preserve what was good about my past in the folds of their fabric and the smells of their antique wood grains. Today, when I laugh, I hear glimmers of who I once was—a funnier me, a lighter me, an unbroken me. Most days I think she's gone, but when I listen to our heirloom clock, I feel strangely connected to this younger me. Me before motherhood. Me before tragedy.

CHAPTER 5:

A GOOD YEAR

(1997)

After graduating from college in 1993, I moved to Wyoming with my fiancé, Ben, who I dated throughout college. We bought a house and started adult life. He was in graduate school, and I took a job as an administrative assistant at a manufacturing company, relieved to find any job at all. It was a stark lesson to learn that a degree from a prestigious university, even as an honor student, did not guarantee a job in a tall building with glass windows. I never forgot the first and last names of my grade school playmates or the rate of pay from my first job—$8.34 an hour.

We were married the following summer and lived in Wyoming for two years while Ben finished his graduate degree. I was recruited into the world of employment and staffing. It was a move that propelled me toward a twenty-four year career in Human Resources and corporate employee benefits.

Our time in Wyoming was filled with many firsts—from our first house to our first puppy, and from our first Thanksgiving dinner to our first lawnmower. There was an innocence and sentimentality in those early years of marriage spent playing house, and we began our first conversations about when to start a family. My husband and I disagreed on much, but we both agreed it was vitally important to have more than one child.

When I was first trying to get pregnant, things did not start off easily the way I'd thought they would. We had moved from Wyoming to Illinois for Ben's first job out of graduate school, and it was an impressive offer from a large company. We were finalizing an offer on a house, leaving Wyoming behind in my husband's old 4x4 truck with a U-Haul trailer in tow. His new company had offered a generous relocation package, and professional packers had come to wrap up everything we owned and take it to Illinois in a giant moving truck. We were both accustomed to the anonymity of city life, and we were stunned to watch our new Illinois neighbors descend on us from across the street and around the corner, bearing hot casserole dishes. One husband even came with a hand truck and moving blankets ready to help us unload. It was a serene Midwest neighborhood with houses set apart by an acre and a half each, allowing for some privacy that Ben and I found comforting.

"Hellooooo!" I heard a booming voice behind me, while directing a gentleman from the moving company down the metal truck ramp.

I turned around to see a short but sinewy man in a white t-shirt with dirty tweed pants held up only by suspenders. He donned an old-world cap and worn-out boots, and while his three-day beard was showing, his ruddy cheeks were cleanly scrubbed, and he wore a welcoming smile.

"Hello there, neighbor!"

I quickly sized him up once it was clear that he was coming over whether or not I invited him, and he was coming with food—an ochre plate covered with dish towels. I walked to meet him halfway at the wood and metal clothesline on the side of the house we were now sharing with his property. *Odd, I didn't remember that eyesore being in any of the real estate photos.*

"Hello. It's lovely to meet you," I replied with my warmest smile, noting that as he got closer, he was not as clean as he appeared from afar.

"Marian. Marian is my name. And who are you, beautiful lady?"

I extended my hand to shake his and thanked him for the introduction. "I'm Jenny. My husband and I just moved here from Wyoming."

Marian was so animated that I half expected him to pull out an accordion and begin dancing to a rousing sea chanty. His accent was strong and like none I had ever heard. Behind him I could see their basement door open, and a pretty woman in her late 50s with auburn hair was coming out to join us. She was followed by an elderly lady who I guessed was in her mid to late 80s. The woman, presumably his wife, looked back to watch the older lady walk out onto the uneven grass before she joined Marian and me. Were it not for the hint of pattern in her kerchief, the grandma looked as if she'd stepped out of a formal mass in a basilica in Eastern Europe. I loved meeting new people, but I had to admit they looked a bit like time travelers from the early 1900s who had landed in our shared field straight from Ellis Island.

"We bring you donuts! Everybody loves the donuts, yes?" Marian's voice projected across the yard. There was no asking if I'd like the donuts or if anyone had an allergy. It was obvious that to decline their food offering would be an insult.

"Thank you so much. Wow! These are beautiful. Did you make them?" I was intrigued and lifted the edge of the towel and tin foil to peek as politely as I could. The sweet smell of sugar and hot oil escaped the cover. They were still warm.

Over the first days and weeks in our new house, our neighbors told us they were from Romania and were proud "citizens of America." They were generous with their time and any tool we needed. We invited them in to see the house, and soon after, Marian began to easily lure Ben over in the evenings with backyard bonfires and some type of clear homemade brew that I later saw was made in the basement. They were fast friends, and I was enjoying learning about their style of cooking from his wife, who had a thick accent but spoke excellent English. Grandmother and I always waved and smiled upon my coming and going, but she never spoke a word of English. It didn't take long before she was my favorite character from next door. Her cheeks were also rosy like Marian's, and though it appeared that she didn't change her selection of clothes, she was clean and never let a strand of hair stray from under her kerchief. We began a game where each time I'd see her she would motion for me to stop and not move. She would disappear into the house and return each time with another ochre plate of homemade donuts. I could never refuse the way her eyes would crinkle at the edges into crescent shapes, and her strong hand on my arm felt reassuring, as she would insist without words that I take the plate.

Our forward neighbors from Europe were curious about why we didn't have any children. We attempted to explain that we had only been married a little more than two years, but they looked at us as if the math didn't make sense. Marian would tease Ben about how he had better get busy and "make some babies," and after we'd been in the neighborhood several months, I was gifted with a large stock pot of soup with spices and herbs that were good for fertility. I couldn't stomach eating the soup without knowing what was in it, but it did trigger me to become more worried about why I was not yet pregnant after we had decided I should stop taking birth control pills two months before. I didn't yet have a primary care doctor, and this was an important reason to get established with someone, so I scheduled an appointment for the following week.

Another month passed and my new doctor couldn't pinpoint why we were not yet pregnant, and she ordered labs that indicated my estrogen and progesterone levels were extraordinarily low. For an otherwise healthy twenty-five-year-old, it didn't make a lot of sense. My new doctor decided to check my prolactin hormone levels, revealing that my lab values were off the charts in the wrong direction. One explanation for elevated prolactin hormone can sometimes be a pituitary tumor, and an MRI revealed that I had a small benign tumor on my pituitary gland. This kind of tumor causes the secretion of too much prolactin, the hormone responsible for lactation. In other words, my body thought I was already pregnant. In hindsight as we learned about the symptoms of elevated prolactin, things began to make sense. I was relieved that I would not need brain surgery or have to deal with the side effects they said might come with it. The endocrinologist assured me there was a medication that would reduce the prolactin level, restoring other hormone values, at which time we would be able to conceive, ideally, within a few months. The medication used at the time caused severe nausea, but on my morning commute each day, I prayed fervently to a God with whom I'd been distant for a decade, that He might give me a chance to be a mother—a dream that had lived deeply in my heart from the time I was able to rock and diaper my own doll babies.

One morning driving to work, I noticed a faint odor in my old white Audi. This one-part banana, three-parts chemical smell was so distracting that I pulled over to get gas and knelt to look behind the front seats, wildly groping under them in case I'd dropped the contents of a snack or something that made logical sense. After finding nothing, I walked into the gas station mini mart, picked out a cold bottle of Sprite, and cheerfully paid the man for it and for the gas, but I noticed on my way back to the car that I had a sudden and intense need for a bean burrito. At that time, I belonged to the camp of people who believed that breakfast should start out sensibly sweet with fruit, cereal, or a muffin. I was not a biscuits and gravy kind of girl. It was 7:55 a.m., but I began the mental dance between hunger and the risk of being late to work. Assuming there would be no one in the drive-through for a bean burrito at 8:00 a.m., I rolled down my window with the manual hand crank, hoping the nauseating smell would relent. Winding around the on-ramp of I-94, I was three bites into the warm, cheesy goodness of my illicit burrito when a thought like a lightning bolt hit me. Was this a different kind of craving? I couldn't be pregnant, not this soon. I wasn't getting a monthly cycle because of the low hormone levels, so how would I know? I'd dealt with daily nausea on the commute for two months as a side effect of the new medication, so how was I supposed to differentiate between that and morning sickness?

Even with my responsibilities of overseeing payroll operations, Human Resources, and a rapidly changing health insurance department, the fast pace of work was no match for my racing thoughts of excitement and anxiety. By lunch I had visited the ladies' restroom twice hourly trying to clear my head and convince myself that I was imagining things. I put my head in my hands in the bathroom stall in a fierce attempt to pull it together. My job was a constant series of daily deadlines, but I didn't want to go back to my office. The bathroom door opened, followed by the familiar click-clack of our receptionist's blocky heels.

"Jenny, are you in here?"

I quickly acknowledged her, flushed, and nearly sprinted to the bathroom sink with a big smile but no eye contact. Peggy was a pastor's wife, warm and maternal, but uncompromising about her values. I loved her dearly, but her uncanny ability to look right through me was disconcerting.

"Are you feeling okay?" That was all she needed to say to trigger an apology and a confession about my bean burrito and Sprite breakfast. As I listened to her asking me the obvious questions about urinary frequency, nausea, and irritability, I secretly used the insides of my upper arms to squeeze against my chest without looking too odd, and it confirmed that my bra area was in fact sore.

How had I not noticed this?

Abandoning my professional boundaries, I found myself talking to her rapid-fire like an old friend, disclosing my newly found pain, and how it made sense that I hadn't noticed since breast pain was one of the symptoms of elevated prolactin. Had the odd aroma in my car been hints of morning sickness or the heightened sense of smell I'd heard about in pregnancy?

"Peggy—do you think I could be pregnant?" She let me jump up and down, and we hugged until she took me firmly by both shoulders to steady me.

"Stop at the pharmacy on the way home and get a test. Stay calm and remember to breathe."

Ben wasn't home when I got there at 5:30, so I fed the dogs to avoid a tongue lashing. I dropped my purse while kicking off my 1990s tan pumps, and I spanned the hallway with two awkward running leaps.

"Not the master bathroom. I might forget something!" I yelled into the empty house.

Wildly irrational, I settled on the hall bathroom as the best spot for a pregnancy test, a two-pack kit. The eggshell paint of that windowless water closet seemed to have a dull yellow haze to it I hadn't noticed before. It felt like my senses were bionic, as I tried to follow the instructions on a package insert the size of a U.S. map. I had served as copilot on a pregnancy test with a friend before, but this time there was no chance of a calm approach. I stood in front of the tiny and dated plastic countertop with marble swirls not daring to look at myself in the mirror. I felt like I was walking on ice where one wrong move could undo this daydream. I had never wanted something so deeply in my life. Could it be possible that I might get to be in the pregnancy club with my best friend and my two neighbors who were also expecting? Things had been so disappointing that year with some mild but nagging medical problems and now a brain tumor that threatened to impact my fertility. I didn't breathe for the entire three minutes required for the test to develop. I stared at the blue control line willing it to reveal a second line. This was torture! *Walk away*, I thought. I turned to face the towel bar, butterflies building in my stomach with ferocious intensity. Waiting longer than three minutes, I stood up on my tiptoes to look down on the test kit, as if that might change the complexity of reading something so simple. It was there. The second line was there.

"What? No way! This can't be possible." I was reminded of Peggy's advice to breathe.

I threw open the bathroom door in a quest for cooler air. I scurried around the bedroom looking for tasks to burn off the nervous energy. *Pick up the clothes on the floor. Put them in the hamper. Put the toothpaste back in the master bathroom drawer.* I was too excited to calm down before taking the second pregnancy test. Back to the hall bathroom—*no wait, check the driveway first to make sure he's not home yet.* The coast was clear. *Face the towel rack again for good luck.* I forgot the tip toe technique this time, but three minutes later there it was in blue on white—two lines. Two lines that would change my life, our lives, forever. I started to cry but then asked myself why.

What do I do now? Okay. I don't want to tell Ben or Mom until I'm sure, so that means not until I see a doctor. I'll call in the morning. How long will it take to get an appointment?

I had to tell someone, or I was sure I couldn't come down from the most intense high of my life. I didn't have to think about who I wanted to tell first before my husband and parents. I gathered every scrap of evidence and put the two tests in a shoe box in the top of my closet. I collected the trash back into the pharmacy bag and grabbed my purse, nearly twisting my ankle on the wood front entry putting my shoes back on. I sped down the country road from our house, past the dairy farm on my right and the old ranch with hundreds of daffodils, long since bent over to the ground from an early spring, before I realized I had better slow down. I couldn't risk being in a car accident. I had a huge job in front of me, and for the next nine months perhaps my body mattered more than I'd ever considered. I'd have to eat right and try to reduce my stress and be careful not to fall if there was a Midwest ice storm.

It was warmer than usual for early May, and it was humid. The inside of the pay phone booth was a sauna, and I was sweating from the sprints around the house in my hysteria. There was something sticky on the phone handset, but I didn't care. I frantically fed quarter after quarter into the slit of the pay phone's mouth, while an automated message screamed that I had twenty minutes of phone credit available. One ring. Two rings.

Oh, no. She won't be home from work yet, I worried.

Then there it was. The comforting voice of my best friend answered, "Hello."

"Ella, it's me."

I was relieved to only wait one day for an appointment to get established with an OB-GYN office, and they confirmed the pregnancy with a standard blood test, scheduling an ultrasound for the following week. Ben wasn't the kind of guy to respond to the news of our pregnancy like an actor in a Hallmark movie, but I gauged his excitement by the number of long-distance phone calls he made to friends telling them the news. He told me he was excited for when the baby would be old enough to take fishing or on other outdoor adventures. I made my peace with his response by knowing that I had the "baby" years covered, and that once our child arrived, he would likely be surprised by a bond unlike any other.

My parents arrived the following week for their annual spring trip, and although it was hard to keep the secret, we held off telling them we were pregnant until they were with us in person. I wrapped up a pair of tiny newborn socks I couldn't resist buying at the hospital gift shop after my first prenatal appointment. They were yellow with a tiny brown bear appliqué and had little no-slip rubberized bottoms, which struck me as silly to think of a newborn's risk of tripping on a slick floor. My mom sat in a kitchen chair across from our blue and white gingham couch, opening the gift bag. She held up the wee yellow socks, looking confused, and then looked at me for explanation.

"What are these for?"

It was fun to watch the shock and surprise come over her face. Ben and I had been married for nearly four years, but she didn't seem entirely ready to be called "Grandma." As it began to sink in for my parents, Mom and I were impressed by the ironic family history that we were both married at twenty-two and both became pregnant at twenty-six.

When we called Ben's parents to tell them the exciting news, his mom and I continued the conversation for another hour after the boys had hung up.

"What about the name Lily?" My mother-in-law put it forward with confidence, followed by her charming giggle.

I was standing by a small pressboard bookshelf in the kitchen where we kept the portable phone.

"I love that! It's classic and would sound rather proper with our last name—quite English. So cute for a little girl."

It felt like confirmation that my mother's intuition might have been right to think we were having a girl. Ben didn't want to know. He wanted it to be a surprise, and part of me wanted that too, so I respected his wishes in spite of wanting to find out for practical reasons, like decorating the nursery.

1997 was a priceless year, filled with the excitement of pregnancy, anticipation of being a mother, and a deep heart connection that was forming with my baby. I was already longing to meet her. I had a strong inclination that she was a girl, but we had also listed some boy options on our list of baby names. The pregnancy was a blend of sharp contrasts. On one hand, it was filled with animated chatter with girlfriends, shopping trips to baby stores, the anticipation of each prenatal office visit, satisfaction found in a job and coworkers I esteemed and loved, and the fun of painting and decorating the nursery. But these highs were tethered to the earth by an ache for Ben to be more involved, for him to accompany me to the doctor's visits, and for him to want these things without being pushed. I was accomplished at compartmentalizing my joy into neat little packages of a life lived without him. It felt as if the baby and I lived in our own reality of connection and glee that I understood Ben couldn't fully participate in without carrying the baby himself. No matter how much I minimized his absence at social events or doctor's appointments, I carried out most of the pregnancy and preparation alone. I was sad that I couldn't fold him into the fun I was having. In the midst of my elation, I was lonely. The wait from the eight-week to the fourteen-week ultrasound felt like an eternity, and there would be no other ultrasound if everything looked good. My OB-GYN asked if I'd like to find out the sex of the baby at the ultrasound, but I told the tech we wanted it to be a surprise.

"The baby looks great," she said as she began narrating the details of basic fetal anatomy. She seemed focused on a particular area of my belly, pushing hard enough that it became uncomfortable.

"So, I'm trying to see if the baby will open its legs a bit more or if I can get a look from underneath. Oh, definitely not a boy! She just showed herself in full glory," the tech exclaimed.

"Ah, eek. We didn't want to know the sex."

"Oh, dear! I'm so sorry, Mrs. Harper."

"It's fine. No worries. I've had a feeling all along that it's, I mean she, is a girl. My husband doesn't want to know, so I'll keep it a secret."

"Well, it's not 100% accurate, so you can't be entirely sure, right?"

After she left the room, I adjusted my clothes and gathered my things, and I stopped to take a deep breath. Before I tucked this secret back into my mind, I took a moment to let the news settle into my heart. I felt like I wanted to cry, but I stopped myself. I knew it would be a mix of happy tears and a feeling of being alone in the pregnancy. I didn't allow the thought to stay, and I returned to the happiness of my maternity.

A girl. She's a girl. Lily, I thought. A half syllable of a laugh escaped from my throat. I had been excited before, but this day made her impending arrival so tangible, so real.

She was right. My mother-in-law had not only predicted correctly, but she had named her granddaughter-to-be. Yellow clothes were already streaming in from the UPS man who frequented our driveway, but I didn't care. I liked yellow. It was cheerful, and I left the doctor's office that afternoon feeling lighter than air. I extended my time off from work by an extra hour and took myself on a quick date to get something to celebrate—an ice cream cone for one, but really for two —Lily and me.

CHAPTER 6:

TWO STRANGERS

(May 2000)

While my first pregnancy was an experience that cannot be duplicated because it was my first, I knew what to expect as I held another dual pack of pregnancy tests in early 2000.

We had moved from outside of Chicago to a bedroom community of Seattle for Ben's next job. As I stared at the positive pregnancy indicators marked in blue on each of the urine sticks, I wanted to fast-forward to the second and third trimesters to get past the worry and anxiety that had been my companion when pregnant with Lily. I dismissed the anxiety of my first pregnancy as normal for a first-time mom and likely due to what they called "pregnancy-induced sleep disorder." I'd struggled with sleep issues since college, but pregnancy made sleep much harder. Ben often referred to the baby as "the alien," and when he did, it made me feel anxious rather than elated. Braxton Hicks contractions arrived early in my first pregnancy and added to my hypervigilance, causing me worry and concern about premature labor.

By week ten of my second pregnancy, I was ready to get out my pregnancy books again and sign up for fun online pregnancy calendars that could tell me each day how the baby was developing. I hoped that these positive activities would be a pleasant distraction the second time through the maternity journey.

During an ultrasound at seven weeks to confirm the status of the pregnancy, I was excited to see the little lima bean on the screen, blinking regularly as if it contained a tiny flashlight. Our second child was due on November 11, 2000 according to both the ultrasound and my calendar. I began policing my every move, from what I ate and drank to how I positioned myself to sleep. As each week passed, I thought I'd worry less and that I'd eventually have the confident and carefree attitude that was characteristic of my friends' second pregnancies.

I hadn't gained much weight, but the obstetrician thought it was likely due to nausea. I was queasier this time than I'd been with my first pregnancy, and Dr. Parr wanted me to take progesterone to protect the baby due to my elevated level of prolactin hormone. I had some minimal bleeding at twelve weeks, and after that I was terrified. I scarcely wanted to pick up a shoe box, let alone my two-year-old. I got in to see the doctor within a day, and he declared all was well. He said it was due to me forgetting to take my progesterone for two nights because we'd had out-of-town guests, and I was busy fussing over company. We were set to sail through the pregnancy, and we began making plans for our second baby's arrival. The only-child curse had been broken, and marital stressors aside, I was ecstatic.

I thought about the baby twenty-four hours a day, seven days a week, whether I was lying awake in bed or dreaming about watching Lily hold her new sibling for the first time. I planned how to fix up a new nursery and began packing a few items to move Lily to her new big girl room. I bought maternity clothes with my mom to supplement my already ample wardrobe. I picked up a used baby name book, and we made a short list of names we were considering for girls—Lilah, Caitlin, Molly, Margaret, and Tess. For boys, we liked Carter, Mason, Mitchell, and Timothy. By twelve weeks, I was showing a bit to those who knew me well, but things were much the same as they were with Lily. The intense nausea that kicked off this pregnancy disappeared like clockwork at twelve weeks, which was a welcome relief. There was a lingering worry about the pregnancy I couldn't pinpoint that wouldn't leave me, despite the weeks that rolled by uneventfully. By fourteen weeks, I gave in to temptation and bought a couple of onesies from the children's consignment store where I was working part-time. I packed away my regular clothes and decided to quit being superstitious and start organizing. The chance of losing a pregnancy in the second trimester was only 2-3%, and I felt alive and hopeful, wearing a glow in my cheeks, especially in my favorite yellow maternity shirt. I met a new friend whose baby was due about six weeks earlier than mine, and we started walking together twice a week, sharing our pregnancies behind dueling jogging strollers.

I wanted so much to tell Lily about the baby. Everyone else I knew told their kids earlier than sixteen weeks, but we thought we'd wait until the second ultrasound when we could find out the gender. We were pleased that our children would be the ideal three years apart. Lily had been asking for a brother or sister before there were any clues, and I resisted telling her. I had my eye on a particular lifelike newborn baby doll at our local toy store to give her as a gift when we told her the big news. The doll was floppy and heavy and felt like a flour sack, and it had a newborn face designed to look real.

In addition to the bleeding, I was plagued by some mild contractions at as early as eleven weeks, and my abdomen would get tight if I did too much of anything. I found this frustrating while trying to keep up with a toddler, and it perpetuated the odd sense of worry. I chalked it up to the same early tightness I'd experienced with my first pregnancy at about twenty weeks, prompting me to cut back to thirty hours a week at work. I tried to make it a point to lie down during part of Lily's naps, and I tried to force myself to rest for brief stints on the couch when I felt achy. I knew it was common to experience aches and pains and unusual sensations of tugging and pulling, as ligaments and tendons stretched in response to pregnancy and a growing abdomen. The pregnancy books reassured me that many systems in my body were changing in preparation for labor and delivery, and I welcomed the distractions of chores and keeping Lily busy and engaged, learning how to count, sound out letters, and learn all of her colors ahead of schedule. She was a curious and verbal child, and we kept active by going to the park, having playdates with her cousin, and preparing for co-op preschool to start in the fall.

I couldn't contain my excitement when the sixteen-week ultrasound date finally arrived, and the timing of my parents' visit was great so they could watch Lily and share in the joy with us. I set aside two little outfits for the baby, silently hoping it might be a boy. During the ultrasound, I looked for the few fetal landmarks I knew. The spine looked symmetrical and complete, I saw a hand above the baby's head complete with fingers too tiny to count, I saw the rhythmically beating heart, and I even recognized the black circle in the middle of the abdomen that I thought was likely a fluid filled stomach. The baby would be still for a few seconds, then bounce about. I could see the outline of a brain inside the cranium, and I focused my gaze on the nose to see if there was any resemblance to my husband or to my daughter's profile. I was so relieved that in my mind we had passed another major milestone and the second half of the pregnancy countdown could begin. I imagined what it would be like to tell Lily the news when we got home, and I could hardly wait to take her to the toy store the next day to get the doll baby I had put on layaway. My thoughts were interrupted by the ultrasound tech silently wiping the gel off my swollen abdomen and handing me a clean white towel. She said she would be right back with the doctor, and I wondered why, but I tried to stay calm, turning to look at Ben who looked worried.

"Everything looked fine, right?" I searched his eyes for any spark of encouragement, but he just looked confused.

"I'm sure it's fine. Wait till they come back and tell us." His often-curt demeanor was strangely comforting, as I looked for anything to grasp that I knew was true.

The ultrasound tech did not return, but soon we were joined by a radiologist in scrubs and a doctor in a white coat. The radiologist flipped on the ultrasound monitor and began scrolling through images captured and recorded by the technician, before she had left me here with a paper blanket and two complete strangers.

"So, from these pictures, it looks like you're having a boy."

Without words he gestured for me to lie down, and he began to neatly tuck the white towel under the band of my underwear. I was suddenly thankful for the matronly appearance of my boring tan maternity underwear, void of lace or pattern, as I lay in the dark with these men suddenly appearing as invested in the baby as I had been for months.

"Did you hear that? He's a boy. You've got your fishing buddy," I narrated.

Ben smiled in the direction of the computer monitor, and while I knew he was hoping for a boy, he quickly wiped away his smile with his hands, now rubbing his forehead. He blushed easily, but as I focused on his face and tried not to turn back to the monitor, his color changed from blushed to red and blotchy.

The radiologist went on. "Tracy called me in to verify a few things she was seeing on the ultrasound, so I wanted to come in and do my own exam if that's okay?"

"Of course," my husband and I replied together as if on cue.

I knew the radiologist would be an M.D., but I squinted to confirm the letters after his name on his badge. Satisfying myself with his credentials, I watched him intently viewing the screen as he deftly rolled the ultrasound wand around my belly, stopping and pressing, then spinning the wand around from other angles as if he was guiding a figure skater across my tight skin. I looked to find excitement in Ben's eyes. I could see him starting to process how real our baby was, and he rubbed his hands across is face again and then nervously through his hair.

"Is everything alright?" my husband asked, his voice cracking the stillness in the room.

The radiologist wiped off the gel from the wand and put it back in its rubber-lined holder next to the giant keyboard.

"I'm definitely seeing some congenital abnormalities in the fetus indicative of a ventricular septal defect, likely the complete absence of an atrial septum, and a very large cyst on the right kidney."

"What are you saying?" I reached out for Ben, and he squeezed back with damp and clammy hands, quickly letting go to point to the ultrasound monitor.

"Umm, I know a fair amount about anatomy, but can you repeat what you are saying and show us on the screen the validation for your findings?" Ben stood up from his chair to lean in closer to the doctors, who were already pressed into the exam room door. It was crowded and beginning to get stuffy.

"Certainly." The previously mute, white-coated doctor stepped forward from the corner and began the explanation, as if hearing it from him would magically make what we heard understandable.

"If you follow me here on the screen, you can see this large fluid-filled sac, where you see the black circle. That is a cyst on the kidney, and you can see how large it is by comparing it to the size of the black circle here, which is the stomach."

"A cyst on the kidney is fixable, right?" I asked in the most professional manner I could gather, as hysteria began to fill my gut like a leaking hot water bottle.

"Well, sometimes, yes. In certain types of small kidney cysts that are simple and benign, we can sometimes see them shrink as kidney development progresses, essentially correcting themselves." Dr. White Coat was finally making some sense, and I liked his answer.

"But…what else were you going to say?" Ben's way of saying *before my hysterical wife interrupted you.*

"Let me show you on the screen. Hang in there with me, Mrs. Harper. We'll get through this together." The radiologist stood up and let the doctor in white take a seat on the universal black vinyl rolling stool.

"The cyst on the kidney is large enough that it alone would be cause for concern, but we are seriously concerned with the baby's heart." I wiped the remaining gel from my stomach with my paper blanket and pulled up my maternity briefs and leggings as far as I could, sitting up to attempt some manner of dignity.

"The fetus, I mean the baby, you can see here in this recording of his heart activity where the red moving out is oxygenated blood, and the blue is deoxygenated blood. He's showing what we call a reduction in ejection fraction. If we compare the video recordings to these still images, we can see a hole in the ventricular septum, or the wall separating the two ventricles from each other."

The radiologist chimed in. "If Doctor Fleming drills down in these images which greatly magnify the heart structures, we can confirm what's called a ventricular septal defect. It's serious on its own, but…"

"There's more?" I interrupted, not meaning to, but I was beginning to sweat and feel dizzy. "My dad's brother died of a heart defect, and my cousin's son died about six years ago too. Is that what this is?"

"There appears to be a defect in the atrial septum as well. In fact, there is no atrial septum. It has not developed. When we see more than one serious congenital anomaly like this, it's likely to be a genetic disorder which links the developmental problems—in this case, the kidney and the two major heart defects. We would need to consider amniocentesis to rule out the strong possibility in this case of cerebral findings—in other words, a problem with development of the head and brain."

"I don't understand. You just came in here and told us we are having a little boy, and the pictures I see look no different than the ultrasound of my first baby, who is healthy. She's two, and we're telling her today that she's going to be a big sister." My voice stopped itself as I choked on congestion.

I hadn't heard myself crying as I spoke, but the doctors became blurry, as my eyes flooded and betrayed me with spilling tears. The radiologist reached for the tissue and handed me the whole box.

I felt alone in my tears, but I looked at Ben, elbows resting on his lap as he rubbed his hands repetitively through his hair at the back of his neck. He was oddly silent.

"So, tell us how you are going to fix him. I mean, this whole building is full of neonatologists and people who do surgery on newborns, and they can even do some surgeries while the baby is still in the womb, right?"

"That's true, Mrs. Harper, both yes and no. The severity of the anomalies we're seeing would result in multiple major interventions and surgeries for this baby immediately in the first few hours and days of life. It is, however, unlikely that the fetus will reach full term in this case."

"Okay, but I've seen stories of babies who've overcome being severely premature in the NICU, and babies with stents and heart surgeries who have lived."

"I know, and those are powerful stories. But in this case and similar cases, the outcome is almost always stillbirth or premature death typically within hours or days."

I cried quietly. What I was hearing was too much to process, and my neck felt like it was being squeezed by an invisible boa constrictor. Ben was talking, but it sounded like he was underwater.

"Yes, we understand. But I have more questions." Ben continued asking detailed questions about fetal anatomy and the prognosis of each condition individually, but he sounded muffled, and I'd taken to staring at the grey rubber door stop on the wall in front of me. It was as if my heartbeat as an expecting mother just stopped. An incomprehensible freight train had collided with my family, with our dreams, with dreams for our second baby—our son. The comfort of numbness began to slide over me like an afternoon shadow, while three men discussed statistics around my abdomen.

Nothing they said registered in my mind until the doctor interrupted my shock with the words that would forever change my life.

"We recommend termination of the pregnancy, what we call therapeutic medical termination due to poor fetal prognosis."

Ben sat down again, this time in silence.

"I'm sorry, what are you saying?" I searched the eyes of both doctors who held my little family in the hands of their advanced degrees and clinical expertise.

"We know this is terrible to hear. I can't imagine what you are feeling right now. This is the difficult part of our jobs. We see cases similar to this about 25% of the time, and in all cases with this combination of fetal malformations, we recommend termination. You are welcome to consult other members of our team, and we can put you in touch with a genetic counselor immediately. The best choice here is the compassionate choice."

I looked to Ben for comfort, for anything I could hold on to. He looked lost, and the usual ruddiness had drained from his cheeks.

"We'll give you some time, and someone will be back to check on you in a few minutes." Dr. White Coat stood up, reaching for the door, and he slid out like an oily sardine in a tin can, making room for the radiologist to nod silently at us as he, too, escaped to the coolness of the hallway.

Give us some time, I thought. I understood how a few minutes was considered a long time, billable time, in the medical field. I stood up to straighten my blouse and necklace only to find my knees buckle under me, and Ben took my shoulders and squeezed. I put my head on his collar bone and cried without regard for anyone else. The world had stopped, and we were the only two parents in it, in that room, in that Seattle skyscraper, in that moment. Two strangers had pulled the pin on a grenade over our lives.

I had spent four months in this pregnant body, and a lifetime preparing for motherhood, and I had filled a giant, beautiful hot air balloon full of expectations and dreams for my baby, only to have these two doctors pop it, letting the pieces fall where they might. They handled it professionally and gave us time to compose ourselves, but I wondered how Ben and I could survive this type of challenge. We'd been through so much, especially in the last two years. This baby had seemed like a beautiful thing for us to rebuild a future around.

"I need to go to the bathroom." I gathered my belongings, handed Ben my jacket, took my purse, and closed the exam door behind me with such a slow and deliberate turn that it didn't make a sound. I needed Ben to see that I had it together, as he was not a fan of waterworks. Around the corner and halfway down the hall I spotted the restroom sign, and I discreetly entered, taking the same care to close the heavy door silently. I turned the sturdy steel lock, and as it clicked into place something broke inside my chest. I doubled over into the pedestal sink and sobbed in a way I never had, wishing I could throw up the lies these doctors were spewing that I couldn't stomach as truth.

I walked alone in a daze from the hospital to the parking garage, rifling through my purse for my misplaced parking ticket, unaware of the downtown commute traffic. I began to worry that the parking attendant at the gate would give me trouble about the lost ticket, and I pictured myself driving straight through the orange barricade if she did. Ben had his motor-cycle, so we drove onto the ferry separately, and I was thankful to make the boat. Ben drove off ahead of me to make arrangements for Lily to go to our neighbors' house so that I could talk to my parents without fear of breaking down in front of her. I walked like a zombie up the four steps to the front door of our house, hearing my angel run to the door, calling "Mommy's home," and my heart lurched.

How could I face her without crying? Would she sense something was terribly wrong?

Motherhood held skills I didn't know I had until that day, and it was the start of learning to tuck my emotions away no matter the situation, like handkerchiefs into invisible pockets. Shock gave me the strength to put on her ivory fleece jacket, the one with little bears donning pink bows, and I coaxed her into her ladybug boots to walk her next door to play with our neighbors' five-year-old son. I felt like I was walking toward a hangman's noose as I made my way back to the house and into the kitchen to tell my parents the news. They already looked pained and prompted me to fill them in.

"The baby," I stuttered. "It's not okay. He's not okay." As I melted into the Formica counter, trying to choke out the details through my sobs, it became more and more real as I told the people who, next to Ben, I was closest to in the world. There was no escaping this once I said it out loud. This was really happening.

My parents were perfect holograms of support, doing and saying all the right things. Ben was on the phone in his office with the door shut, talking to Dr. Parr about more details of our case and how to proceed, and I was glad he was in charge that night. An unknown radiologist had pinned today on the timeline of our lives forever. I heard Ben relaying his conversation with Dr. Parr to my parents. I wandered down the hall toward our bedroom to find some privacy, when I heard Ben tell my folks that there was "more to the story" than just the kidney and heart defects. My socked feet froze in the hall. I was unable to stop eavesdropping, and yet I wanted to plug my ears.

"There appear to be some cerebral skull malformations as well. He mentioned something called a 'lemon sign.'"

I tried to scream but nothing came out. I knew what it meant from the context of our baby's other malformations and the tone of my husband's voice. I felt like a wild animal, as I sunk to the floor against the bed, crying without the social limitations of a public restroom in a large urban hospital. A low pitch that sounded like it was coming from someone else's throat pleaded "no" over and over. I ripped my maternity shirt open and jerked it off my body. A button flew off, hit the mirror and landed on the top of the dresser, but I didn't care. The shirt was from Target and not a fancy maternity boutique, and I knew I could sew the button back on and sell it at the consignment store. I planned to fix my angry mistake even as I did it. I didn't deserve cute maternity clothes. I was no longer in the pregnancy club.

Ben came back to find me in the closet as I continued screaming the word "no" over and over as my knees sank beneath me. There wasn't time for him to catch me, but I felt an awkward hand on my shoulder as my knees bore into the carpet. I functioned normally in front of Lily for the rest of the evening, but after I read her a story and put her to bed, my parents sleeping downstairs, Ben drove us to Safeway at midnight to get a few things, as he hadn't eaten all day. He picked a box of sushi from the cold case by the deli. The market, a place I cheerfully frequented twice a week with my bulging mid-section and gleeful toddler, felt like a fluorescent morgue.

The next day on the phone, our OB talked us through the benefits of doing amniocentesis, whether or not it would help us make our decision now. If we decided to go through with terminating the pregnancy, he felt it might later provide confirmation of our decision to terminate, if a serious genetic disorder was found. His concern was that the results would take up to two weeks, and we felt pressure from him to make a decision within the week to avoid what he alluded to could be additional complicating factors of a second trimester abortion. We were both leaning toward terminating the pregnancy as the least disastrous choice between two terrible alternatives. We were both medically minded, and even if we terminated the pregnancy before the amnio results came in, we wanted to know if there was a genetic explanation for our baby's problems. Ben also thought it would be important to know if this could happen in a future pregnancy. I couldn't think past the next fifteen minutes. The medical team emphasized that the physical malformations were clear on the ultrasound, regardless of the outcome of amniocentesis.

A geneticist was consulted who could not see a clear syndrome evident in our son's problems, further indicating that genetic testing results might come back normal. I was confused but thankful that we seemed to have a united front on the most painful decision of our lives. Amniocentesis, while I had been through other procedures, terrified me. I'd thought they put a huge needle through the belly button, but I was relieved that it was a carefully selected location identified using ultrasound. The needle stick hurt less than I imagined, but it was intensified by the knowledge of why we were doing this and the fear that they might hurt our tiny baby, who had miraculously curled up to one side of the amniotic sac, giving the doctor ample space from which to draw fluid. I fought a strong urge to vomit when I felt the needle hesitate against the layers of muscle and connective tissue and then disappear into my abdomen until it reappeared on the ultrasound screen, greatly magnified. I couldn't turn my head away from watching the needle puncture the amniotic sac as I felt a rush of adrenalin, wanting to jump up from the table and shout, *stop, you're hurting my baby!* They got what they needed and retracted the needle, and I immediately felt my uterus clamp down angrily around the point of entry, now invisible aside from the ridiculous Band-Aid they gave me as a consolation prize. Cramps sprang into action, instinctively doing their job reacting to the foreign object, and I was told it was a normal part of the process. I was advised to take it easy for 24 hours, but I couldn't help but wonder how they imagined I'd be able to sleep as we wrestled with the final decision to terminate our baby's life.

Ben and I spent another night in the living room waiting for the TV to eventually lull me into a coma by 3:00 a.m. When Ben was fully ready to articulate his decision and said he felt sure about taking the doctor's recommendation to terminate, a sense of relief came over me like a prickly hot flash. The grey area could now become black, and anticipatory grieving could begin. I was touched by my rarely sentimental husband who suggested that we name our son, and we agreed upon the name Nathaniel. Our baby had been a wriggling fish in my belly for two weeks already, and he was busy that night. The gleeful movement of our beloved baby felt like a horror movie, and pain pierced my throat each time I felt the quickening. I wanted to hold him, to make him understand, to convince him that I loved him so much that I had to save him from certain death and a lifetime of pain.

But I was only human, and his movements also made me feel physically ill, as I longed to have some escape from a pregnancy that I believed was doomed to end poorly. I felt nauseated by guilt for a decision that had yet to be carried out.

We agreed to call the doctor in the morning to see if we could get on the surgical schedule Friday so as not to endure the weekend in prolonged agony, but to begin the grieving process. Ben wondered if we could have the baby cremated, and I was so thankful to him for bringing it up. We agreed to scatter the ashes somewhere meaningful, like at the family lake house, he suggested, and he made me agree to "nothing permanent," meaning there was to be no gravesite or permanent memorial. He asked me not to "hold a torch" over this. Denial was doing its job to numb us from the full blow, as we somehow survived another long night.

The next afternoon during Lily's nap, I moved into compulsive mode, my go-to state when things felt out of control. I wanted all business in order. I packed my bag, got ready to go to Seattle for a pre-operative procedure, and called the hospital to pre-admit and clear any legal hurdles about cremating such a small baby. I called the local funeral home and, with surprising strength, arranged for them to receive my son's remains. My dad was scheduled to watch Lily so my mom could accompany me to the office visit to have my cervix dilated. She didn't want me to go alone.

The usual excitement of going to an appointment at my obstetrician's office was replaced with anxiety and dread as Mom and I took the elevator in silence. Janice seemed to skip the regular check-in procedure and ushered me to an exam room, her hand gently steering me by the elbow without words. I saw Dr. Parr in his office as I was "roomed," and I could hear him dictating like a monotone zombie while I undressed and put on a gown and rubberized socks. My mom agreed to wait in the lobby, as I was deeply private about medical appointments. No one told us what to expect with the process of cervical dilation, and Dr. Parr was cryptic and began the procedure with little explanation. I pressed my heels into the sheepskin-lined stirrups so hard I didn't realize I'd inched up the back of the exam table and nearly over the top of the flat pillow. It was the only way I could avoid screaming, and I was so embarrassed that someone in the lobby might hear. I knew there were other young moms sitting out there. With the insertion of the first laminaria stick I could not lie still on the table. The laminaria was supposed to trigger the cervical dilation process mechanically as each medical-grade stick expanded over 24 hours.[1]

Dr. Parr grew impatient with me and, one octave short of yelling, he warned me, "If you could just stay still and breathe this would go much more quickly!"

At that I began my usual string of apologies, and I began to cry as quietly as I could. There was a knock at the door before it forcefully opened to reveal a frenzied version of Janice who had left the front desk of the busy office to join us.

"I'm so sorry," I told her. "I didn't mean to cause a problem." Thankfully, she was a nurse inclined toward compassion, and she took a position up near my right shoulder, grabbing my hand like she meant it.

"What about the people in the lobby? Aren't they going to hear me?"

"Don't you worry about that!"

"I can't do this. It's too painful."

"Look," Dr. Parr was stern and direct. "We have two more of these to place into your cervix. It will be over soon, but you've got to cooperate."

"I feel like something's wrong. I can't do this. I just can't!" I was begging. "Can you just take them out, or maybe I can do this under anesthesia or something?"

The nurse squeezed my hand tight. I closed my eyes in an effort to compose myself, and Dr. Parr's tone softened a bit. "Things are really closed, so let's consider only one more and see how that goes." I started to climb up the table to inch away from him.

I had endured my share of physical pain by this point in my life, including childbirth and major surgery, but the pain I felt when Dr. Parr inserted these sterile but foreign sticks of laminaria was like no other. I had no control over my crying out.

"I need you to take deep breaths and come back down from the table and work with me, not against me."

"I can't." I tossed my head from side to side willing myself to be somewhere else, unable to hold back sobs of pain.

There was loud knock at the door. Janice bellowed, "Not now!" The door opened anyway to reveal my mom. Her face was pale, but her cheeks were red.

"I'm her mom. I'm coming in."

Janice looked relieved, and I apologized again, glad she could go back to the patients in the lobby.

There was a dimension to the pain of the procedure that was not only physical but deeply emotional—an instinctive and primitive pain of a mother, trying desperately to protect her baby from harm, wanting to cast out anything foreign. I could no longer tell myself that after this, life would return to normal, because this procedure made it clear to me that it wouldn't. I was certain this was my last chance to save our baby. Dr. Parr dilating my cervix meant there was no turning back. I was doing this. I was letting someone kill my baby. I could not fully grasp it. The ferryboat ride home with my mom was excruciating, and the night was spent squirming and pacing and sleepless. I told myself that at least we were moving forward, out of the grey and into the black. I had no idea just how black the storm clouds were as they formed above us.

CHAPTER 7:

QUICKENING

(June 2000)

The next day, we waited through the two-hour hospital pre-admit process, most of which I spent pacing or attempting to sit on one hip from the excruciating pain of the laminaria dilation process. We were ushered to a private room with a gurney just as forceful cramping finally began. The experience for me was searing and unproductive pain, void of the desired outcome the doctor wanted of uterine cramps associated with early labor. When the pain of cramps finally arrived just an hour before surgery, it was a welcome relief because the pain was at least different, though familiar from having experienced labor before. I closed my eyes there on the gurney and imagined what it should have been like— there at that same hospital where I was scheduled to deliver a healthy baby. I imagined those early labor pains escalating naturally, leading to the delivery of a healthy son. Ben read a magazine and talked only if I drew him out, but I felt desperately alone, clutching Lily's picture I had brought to the hospital as my only comfort. In that interminable hour, I knew that collateral damage was happening to my life and to our marriage. I no longer felt like a young twenty-nine-year-old woman, and part of me wanted to close my eyes forever and just die. I had only recently explored what coming back to God might look like, and I had a virtually nonexistent prayer life. Holding on to the picture of my extraordinarily beautiful little girl was the only thing that kept me tethered to the earth.

A nurse finally called us to go the second stage waiting area, the last stop before the operating room, and we were shocked to be wheeled into one large room that resembled a hotel lobby. It was like a scene from a 1950s day room in a mental institution. I looked around in horror to see that the anonymity of our first private room was now undeniably absent. They pushed my bed into the corner, but there were no curtains, no place to cry in secret. Other same-day surgery patients sat in bleach-faded gowns on couches, reading copies of *People* and *Time* magazine, nervously pretending not to see one another. *How could they do this?* I wondered in a daze. How could they put a woman in my situation covered with nothing more than a hospital gown and a flimsy sheet in the same room with people who had come for laparoscopic knee surgeries and shoulder repairs? I hunched down in my gurney, hoping my private parts weren't on display, feeling like a wet and wounded baby bird. I tried to draw close to the angel inside of me whose life was coming to a close by our own choosing. I hurt physically and emotionally in places I didn't know could simultaneously exist. I folded in on myself as tightly as I could against the hardness of my belly, while our Nathaniel bounced frantically in my stomach, as if trying to tell me he was very much alive. I wanted him to keep moving, and I also wished he would stop. Finally, in desperation, I asked Ben to put his hand on my stomach.

"Make him stop kicking," I said, as this had always worked with our first baby.

As expected, the baby stilled, but I felt I had made Ben uncomfortable. I wanted him to feel uncomfortable, to feel some piece of this visceral terror and to have some final contact with the baby, our baby. He flipped nervously through his magazine, appearing to read, but how could he? I overheard Dr. Parr describe our impending abortion procedure to a technician in scrubs by the nursing station who dared to ask, "How is it done in the second trimester?" I made out the words "curettage" and "break it apart," and the shock of his carelessness made the room pitch above my head as if I was on a ship. I whispered to the God to whom I'd been a stranger for so long, "Please, God. Help me."

I knew Dr. Parr's audible and inappropriate description of how my procedure would be done was a vulgar and vile lack of professionalism, and a violation of my medical privacy, void of any respect for me as a patient or for the life of our unborn baby. Were it not for the pain and the tether of my IV, the rage I felt made me want to jump up from the gurney, grab Dr. Parr by the paper collar of his scrubs and shake him. I was interrupted by another nurse who came in to make sure I was who I claimed to be for hospital legal purposes.

"Do you know why you are here today, Mrs. Harper? Can you tell me what procedure you're having done?" She looked at her clipboard avoiding eye contact with me.

What could I say? I was always professional, always nice, always polite. Her question seemed unnecessary and cruel, but I knew she'd insist that I answer.

"Can I just read what you have written on the consent form and sign it? Please?"

"Hospital policy. I need you to verify your name, date of birth, and, in your own words, the procedure you are consenting to." Now she was looking at me.

"Um. Jenny Harper, August 19, 1973. We are having a D&E, dilation and evacuation, due to poor fetal prognosis of a baby boy who we love and want. Is that enough confirmation for you?"

I had never met this version of myself with a steely jawline, swollen eyes, and no make-up. She was a woman emerging inside me who I both hated and admired.

Ben was a terse and often cold man, and if you crossed him, he could hold a grudge indefinitely, but when they came to get me to go to the operating room, he grabbed my hand. In that moment, I loved him for that. When they made him let go, my tears came hard, and I felt completely alone. I felt sickened by the fact that I'd never been closer to Ben, but that it had come out of this tragedy. The bulky gurney was a new one that had come with the hospital's recent makeover, and it was too big to fit through the door of the surgical suite we were scheduled for, so they asked if I would mind walking into the OR and getting myself up onto the table.

"Um, okay, sure," I replied like a good little patient with a vacant straight-lined smile. Something in my chest felt like it cracked, and any innocence that remained in me was left behind with the abandoned gurney in the hall. I tried to chat cordially with the nurse and anesthesiologist for distraction, but then I saw Dr. Parr, in a blue scrub cap and a yellow paper gown, as his nurse helped him into extra-long surgical gloves. I knew he would never look the same to me, and I suddenly felt cold, as if looking at him was like staring down an angel of death. It took tremendous self-control to voluntarily stay on the operating table, knowing I would soon feel worse than I did before my submission to these strangers in scrubs. I started bawling, and I called out as if it would save my baby who would soon be forever out of my body and out of my protection, no longer sheltered in the safest place. In the final minutes, as panic took over, I wanted to get up and run, but there was nowhere else to be but here. The lights were so bright, but no matter how much my eyes hurt—like staring at the sun—I couldn't look away. It was the only pain less sharp than what I was facing.

I had run out of small talk to exchange with the anesthesiologist and the nurses. The lament of this day was incomparably worse than the regret I held over what I thought was worst decision of my life—not to pursue medical school. It was a ridiculous comparison, but it was all I had to draw from in my life experience until this foreboding day in June. My eyes darted around the operating room, and I marveled at the lack of compassion, as two technicians and two nurses went about their preparations.

How could they not know? How could they be in a hurry?

Someone asked me for my left arm. I knew the drill. I instinctively drew my arm back quickly, apologizing with a gentle, "I'm sorry," before surrendering my arm again. There was no one who could do this, endure this but me. I knew once I was asleep there would be Velcro straps pinning my arm to a board, but for a few more seconds I was still free and within my legal rights to leave. It was the blue disposable shower cap pulled just over my hairline that put me over the edge, and I began to cry again, a stifled cry that turned to weeping until a stern male voice told me to stop crying or I would be too congested for the anesthesia.

"I'm sorry," I whispered again.

A nurse with kind eyes behind her mask wiped the corner of my eyes with a tissue that felt like industrial paper towels, as a disposable rubber mask that smelled like plastic cherries pressed down over my mouth and nose. Finally, the lights began to hurt less and less. The shot into the IV went directly to my primitive animal hindbrain where it began to hurt and sting. I cried out, "I want my baby," and then there was emptiness.

* * *

My father and husband had a strained and unique relationship. My father expected he'd be close to the man I chose to marry and that he'd be gaining a son. My choice in Ben proved to be quite a challenge for him as he struggled to understand and connect with my husband. The two men cautiously played their given roles, but my mother and I had been running interference for years. In 2000, the bottle finally exploded when we found ourselves as grieving parents and grandparents in virtual house quarantine together, caught in a tidal wave of medical drama. My mom could not conceive of the way Ben was handling his grief. When pushed, he preferred to retreat into a haze of solitude and constructive physical work. My parents looked as if they might break open each time Ben chose to do home improvements instead of holding my hand. While Ben and I were both thankful for my mom's help and my dad's loving care of Lily, they thought they should probably "get out of our hair" as Mom put it.

Ben chose to throw himself into major outdoor projects, because he was not one to sit inside on a sunny day, and definitely not with a grieving postpartum woman. I was not yet strong enough to give him the space he needed to grieve in his own way. I wanted to grieve with him, not alone. I had grown accustomed to our emotional separateness, but this was a life-altering experience that I prayed would solder us together and not tear us apart.

As I recovered from the most emotionally charged surgery of my life, my in-laws were due to arrive three days after my parents left so that Ben and my father-in-law could start work on a bathroom remodel. The visit was scheduled to last for ten days, and I thought I might not survive another social visit. I did not want to share my private pain with them or with anyone other than my husband. I was angry that Ben would go forward with the visit in light of the circumstances, and I found it shocking that they still planned to come. I couldn't bear to have them see me out of control and sleep deprived. The afternoon of their arrival, I managed to break my toe in a running leap to keep the cat from throwing up on our off-white carpet. My toe turned black and swelled up, making it impossible to walk, further shortening the leash with which I was attached to the house, my visiting in-laws, and my grief. I excused myself from entertaining them under the guise of taking a shower when I could no longer hold back the tears that came every day.

CHAPTER 8:

FORGOTTEN

(September 2000)

The post-surgical pain lessened after three days but escalated again after the first two weeks while my in-laws visited. After they left, I reached the six-week milestone in my recovery, and we drove south to the lake house. Along the way, I often stared out the window, holding back tears and wincing with pain at every bump in the road. It was emotionally healthy to be away from the house, and it was a pleasant diversion for Ben and a fun time at the beach for Lily. Regardless, my pain worsened each day. I met with Dr. Parr shortly after we returned home and was awarded the diagnosis of a post-surgical uterine infection, a bladder infection, and a kidney infection. Two antibiotics and a script of pain pills later, I limped from his office with his unpleasant hypothesis that the cells he saw in my urine could also be indicative of kidney disease. The pain improved after a few days of antibiotics, and I was reassured. By the end of the week, however, the pain had moved to my lower back, and I asked for a urine re-check. It was still not cleared up, and they put me on a more appropriate third antibiotic. I was re-checked again by Dr. Parr the following week, who pronounced things improved, and I drove home confused by the continued uterine pain. Two weeks later, after I'd pleaded for another appointment, Dr. Parr examined me and told me that he palpated a lump in either the colon at the level of the cervix or between the two organs. My physical reserves were waning, but I swallowed hard and searched his face.

"Are you saying the lump could be cancer?"

"Too soon to tell until we get the pathology back on the cells I collected, and then we'll just check it again next month." He tossed his exam gloves into the steel medical waste bin and spun his chair away from me and over to the computer.

"I'm still in a lot of pain, and I'm trying to keep up with my daughter. I'm not sure how to process the idea of waiting that long to know what's going on?" He looked up, then hesitated before speaking.

"I'll order an ultrasound for Monday, and we'll go from there."

As I folded laundry on the bed Sunday afternoon before the scheduled ultrasound, Lily playing happily at my feet with her miniature keyboard, fear began to creep into the back of my mind.

What if it was cancer?

There was no way I could get sick or die, leaving my little girl without a mother. I told myself that cancer was unlikely, and I explained it away, feeling certain it was just inflammation from the D&E surgery twelve weeks prior.

Monday morning, I found no comfort in flipping through an out-of-date *Southern Living* magazine in the medical tower of one of Seattle's leading hospitals. I looked at my watch to find it was 2:15 p.m. and my ultrasound appointment was set for 2:00 p.m. I pressed down hard on the whitewashed wood of the chair's armrest to stand up as gracefully as I could despite the gnawing pain that was my constant companion.

"Hi, is everything okay with my appointment or maybe I got the time wrong?"

"Oh, sure. Let me look in the system to see where they're at back there." She bit her lower lip while scanning the monitor.

"I see. They're just running behind with the patient before you. But you're in the queue next, so it shouldn't be too long."

"Oh, okay. I just can't reschedule since it's a two-hour commute for me each way, and I have to do this today." No idea why I was oversharing, I apologized and reassured her that I was fine waiting.

"Thank you for checking." I smiled and walked carefully and silently in flats in another unnecessary gesture of apology.

I obediently returned to my seat, strategically chosen with a view of the door where the ultrasound tech had come to get me last time. Last time.

Should I have changed my OB-GYN? I thought.

Dr. Parr had traumatized me during more than one office visit and procedure, and it had taken two months to get him to take the post-surgical pain seriously, with his only response three courses of antibiotics and a proposed cancer diagnosis.

Why had it taken so long to get an ultrasound when it seemed the most conservative approach?

I looked out to my left to the bay of windows along the waiting room wall which overlooked Elliot Bay and the Seattle shipping lanes. It offered a temporary distraction.

A recipe toward the back of the magazine showed a country lake house adorned with banners of red, white, and blue, and a linen-draped table covered in blue hydrangeas boasted a huge sheet cake decorated like an American flag using blueberries and raspberries. It reminded me of our house in the suburbs of Chicago. I glanced back to the large orange cranes along the waterfront and was transported in a vivid daydream to our simple but sweet, all-American ranch style house in Illinois. Just after New Year's Eve of 1996, Ben was adamant that we have a litter of puppies with our gorgeous male yellow lab and our sweet and gentle female black lab, but unfortunately our dogs were unable to get pregnant easily. My mind replayed the embarrassing trip to a veterinary fertility specialist who checked our male dog first, where we had the awkward opportunity to look at his "little swimmers," as the vet called them under a microscope. His fertility was definitely not the problem, but rather it was his "technique." I found the whole canine reproductive process nauseating, once I learned how they were going to obtain what they needed from our boisterous young male, and the thought of our poor girl being artificially inseminated made me lightheaded. They reassured us that this happened sometimes. I just wanted to go wait in the car. Shortly after we arrived home from the veterinary specialist, our male dog suddenly had all the right moves. We'd invested a big sum of money seeing the vet that day, and Ben was less than amused.

Sixty-three days later, I took a call from Ben while working in my Chicago office. He thought our female dog was acting strange, so maybe this was labor. I couldn't wait to get home, and I called the vet to describe her disinterest in food and water, her panting, and her pacing, and they confirmed it was time. It seemed she was in labor for at least four or five more hours before she finally agreed to lie down in the whelping box Ben had made for her in the garage. We'd set up a heater, a shop lamp, and everything we thought she might need. Once the first puppy arrived, it was only about fifteen minutes until the next wet and shiny baby made its arrival, still covered by the amniotic sac until Penny licked each puppy clean. The new babies had steam coming off of their hot, wriggling bodies in the cold of an early spring Chicago night. All six of the puppies whimpered and screeched and whined, tossing their heads about wildly as they searched for something warm. Penny looked terrible. Her eyes were bloodshot, and her lower eyelids hung down pink and dry. She continued panting though it had been over an hour since the arrival of the sixth pup. I couldn't help myself, so with clean hands, I guided a few of the lost puppies to the teat to nurse and to get warm with their brothers and sisters. Five latched on tightly and were nursing well, but the sixth little pup flopped its head from side to side not making a connection with the available nipples near him. This pup didn't cry as much as the other babies, and I began to worry. As I studied the newborn, I noticed he was nearly a third smaller than the other puppies, and I confirmed it was a boy. Each time I put his little nose right up to the teat, he tossed his head back and lost contact. I ran inside to get

Ben, thinking we might have to take him and the whole lot of them to the vet. When I came back with Ben, the runt was in the corner of the box alone and crying with a more fervent voice.

"Oh no. She's not getting him! What do we do?"

He sat down on the bucket by the dog box and lifted the baby up with a towel to put it back up by the nipples closest to Penny's tail, hoping she wouldn't notice him innocently eating. A repetitive and tireless exercise began each time our mama dog lifted her head to sniff around the puppies, licking each tiny head until she paused at the suckling runt. Her sniffing hastened, and she nudged the helpless pup onto his back, rolling him away with her nose. It was a heartbreaking sight. I coached her, I comforted her, and I cried until nearly 4:00 a.m., but I never thought to pray. My dog, Penny, wanted to please me more than her instincts, and as time passed, she let him suckle just long enough for him to get the hang of it. His head was noticeably bigger than the other five puppies, but he moved well.

Exhausted and knowing I had to get up for work in less than three hours, I stood up quietly and carefully hoping she would let the struggling little runt stay. As I turned around to tiptoe away to check the heater and dim the lights, I heard the familiar panicked bellow of a puppy losing its hold on Penny, and I turned around to watch the runt topple over the others in the pile of wet velvet heat. I froze where I was standing. I knew I couldn't watch her rejection of the sick baby one more time. I thought I should probably walk away and let nature run its course, at least for a few hours. I had cried so much and was exhausted, but I wiped my sleeve across my face yet again as I tried to let go and trust our dog to do her job. I made it to the door into the house before I took one last look. I began counting the puppies. Two were making snorkeling sounds, paired off sleeping against each other for warmth. There were two more asleep against Penny's belly kicking their little pink feet as if they were running in place. *Where were the others?* There was one under her tail camouflaged, but that was only five. *Where was he?* I made the two leaps back to the wooden whelping box where Penny lay under the lamp, and as my eyes darted all around her bedding, I found him utterly alone facing away from his mama and littermates, scarcely moving.

"Penny, no!" Her collar rattled as she jerked her head up to look at me in fearful submission. I rubbed the nearly lifeless and chilled baby against me with a towel and held him close for warmth. Immediately there was squirming at my neck and I burst into tears upon hearing his tiny squeaks and pops.

"Listen, girl. This is your baby." I held his tiny face to her nose. "He's a good boy, and you're a good mama." Penny licked him across the head causing him to bellow.

"I'm going to put your baby where he belongs, back with you. Now, leave it!"

I wasn't sure if my utterance of "please, God" constituted a prayer, but I had nothing left to give. I dropped off to sleep for what felt like five minutes before my alarm went off and I trudged back out to the garage, not stopping to get socks or slippers. I felt sick from the nerves of worry and lack of sleep.

"Jenny?" The sound of my own name jerked me out of my daydream and back to the Seattle waiting room.

"Yes," I replied quickly, gathering my purse and sweater so she could see I would not keep her waiting. The nurse ushered me to a small exam room that was only two doors down from where we had received the worst news of our lives about the serious birth defects of our baby boy. This room looked exactly the same, except that the exam table, sink, and cabinets were reversed. She asked me intake questions, took my blood pressure and pulse, told me to undress from the waist down, and handed me a hospital gown. Something about the feel of the black, textured surface of the pull-out step to the table gave me a sharp stab in my stomach. I grabbed the paper-lined table to steady and reorient myself. This was not June 2; it was September 4, and I wasn't here to check on the progress of my baby's gestational age or to get one of the new three-dimensional ultrasounds. He was gone. Nathaniel was gone, and I had yet to fully wake up from the nightmare. I tucked the paper under my right hip and then under my left, in an effort to ensure that every inch of my untanned legs was covered. It had been a long commute, and I was still in a great deal of pain, stooping over slightly when I walked to avoid a burning tightness I felt if I stood up straight.

"Jenny?" A different nurse in scrubs poked her head into the exam room. I looked up from the tear in my paper lap blanket to acknowledge her with a warm smile, in spite of last night's fight with Ben.

"We'll be right in. It's been one of those days. We're so sorry to be running behind."

"Oh, no problem at all." I rarely said what I meant. The door closed with the sound of a metallic click, and I was once again left alone with my thoughts.

I closed my eyes and blinked hard to avoid crying. The pain of sitting up on the rigid exam table was becoming unbearable, and I willingly traveled back again in my mind to the kitchen of our Illinois house. I smelled coffee, as I opened the door to the garage to find my husband holding the runt puppy.

"Is it him? Is he dead?" I felt my throat tighten as it always did before I cried.

"He looks better." It was such a relief to cry this time out of joy, as I knelt by Penny and patted her smooth head. When Ben put the pup down, he rooted around aggressively for a nipple, oblivious to the unnaturally large size of his head.

"It's a miracle! She did it!"

"Don't you think *he* did it?" Ben corrected. I was too exhausted for an argument. I lowered my knee onto the cold concrete and bent over to kiss our sweet dog on the head.

"Thank you, girl."

As the story of our puppies played behind my eyes in that exam room in the neonatal imaging department, I understood where this memory had come from.

Was I like our mama dog who rejected her baby because it wasn't perfect or because she instinctively knew it was sick? Of course not, I thought, in an attempt to let myself off the hook from the delayed grief processing that regularly crept in.

This game of comparison, even to the family dog, was the start of comparing my worth to every mother I knew or met. Ben and I were humans—humans with advanced medical science. We had a team of experts advising us about the kind of suffering our baby might expect were he to live. Penny was a dog. We were people—parents faced with an impossible choice. We were told termination was the compassionate choice. Yet as I replayed the memory of our dog rejecting her puppy on that cold Midwest night, it looked anything but compassionate. She hadn't been willing to expend the resources to feed her sick puppy. *What was our excuse? What made me any better?* In the end, she had been persuaded to keep her puppy. *Why did no one persuade us?*

I startled at the sound of the ultrasound room door opening again. Another new face came in, still rubbing her hands from the foam alcohol dispenser just outside the door.

"Hi, I'm Dr. Helsik. I'll be doing your pelvic ultrasound. Do you have any questions?"

"Um, no. Well, yeah, I guess I'm just lucky to have a doctor today. That's not how this usually seems to happen."

She could tell I was asking a question more than making an observation, and she was quick to respond warmly and with reassurance.

"I know you've been through this before, but that's very observant. Our tech reviewed your chart and came to get me, so you wouldn't need to undergo the ultrasound, then wait for her to show it to me before you could leave." She busied herself moving the bottle of ultrasound gel from the warmer next to the wands of various sizes.

"Okay, well I'm sure that's good. Thank you."

"If you could lie back, we'll tuck this paper into your underwear, so I don't get gel all over you. "

"Oh, they told me to take off my underwear. Did I not need to?" I closed my legs around the unforgiving paper in an effort to better cover up.

"That's absolutely fine. We'll start with a standard ultrasound to ensure everything looks okay, and only do a transvaginal ultrasound if we have to, as I saw in the chart that you've been in a lot of pain since June. Is that right?"

"Um, yes. I had surgery June 2, and nothing's been right since then. Ongoing spotting, pain that just hasn't gone away since, uterine infection, antibiotics."

"I'm so sorry you've been through all that." She squeezed the warm jelly onto my stomach, more than I was used to seeing, and I tried to relax my legs a bit now that unspoken female confidentiality had been established. I put my left arm over my head as instructed to "stretch out a bit."

"Ovaries are measuring within normal size." I wasn't used to hearing a play-by-play of my anatomy since the techs were usually limited about what they could say, leaving patients to wait for a later phone call or a report in the mail.

"Your cervix looks closed and back to pre-pregnancy status. Measuring your uterus now. Perfect width." She paused, clicking more buttons on her screen and scrolling rapidly with the roller ball on her keyboard.

"Did you have any pain like this before the D&E in June?"

"No. Never. Everything was fine."

She squinted her eyes and adjusted her glasses, followed by more clicking and screenshots when she took the wand off my belly and wiped it clear of gel.

"I printed two of these images for my colleague in the room next door. I'll be back in just a minute."

"Wait," my voice squeaked as I called out to her, not meaning to. "No, sorry. It's fine. No problem."

She was back in a few minutes, and I hesitated to greet her with my eyes since I was lying down taking some comfort in the perfect grid of squares over the fluorescent lights on the ceiling.

"You can sit up if you'd like." She grabbed my hand to help me up. I fixed the torn paper back under my hips.

"So, the good news is, we don't need to do the transvaginal ultrasound, so we're done. But I do have some findings that explain the post-surgical complications and infection." She took care to keep her eyes squarely on me.

"Is it cancer? Oh, God. I have a two-year-old." I had just endured one of the longest weekends of my life trying to reconcile Dr. Parr's hypothesis of cervical cancer.

"No. It's not cancer. But you do have what we call POC." My mind immediately jumped to something like Polycystic Ovarian something... *What did the last letter mean? Couldn't be that.*

I asked if I could start getting dressed while I listened, but her face grew drawn as her voice became quieter, softer, as if she had a secret to tell.

"I'm so sorry, Mrs. Harper. POC is what we call 'products of conception,' and what I see on the ultrasound is called 'retained products of conception.'"

"I'm sorry, what?" I understood what she said but I didn't understand that it was happening to me.

I slid off the exam table, wrapping the paper behind me and turning to face her and the ultrasound screen she had failed to turn off. I couldn't stop myself from looking at the outline of my abdomen in plain sight. Within the broken white outline of my pear-shaped uterus, I saw it. Perhaps if I had I not experienced so many ultrasounds by this point in my life, the abstract lines, arches, and circles might have been foreign to me. It would have been a welcomed mercy from what I saw over her shoulder. There in the center of my uterus was a small cluster of matter, white lines and tiny white dashes, and for a second, I was sure I saw vertebrae. I looked away to search her face as I reached behind me for the sink to hold myself up.

"Are you okay? Why don't you sit down for a minute?"

Sit down? I can't sit down, I thought to myself as my symptoms began to make sense.

"Is your husband here in the lobby?"

"No."

"You live far away, right? I don't think you should commute alone."

"So, wait. Are you saying that part of my son is still inside me? That's why I've been so sick?"

"Well, the baby is not living, so please don't worry about that. Our concern is for you and your health."

"How did this happen? How could Dr. Parr have made this mistake?" I continued. "Didn't he use an ultrasound when they did the D&E?"

"I don't know. He most likely did, but it's not always required," she mediated.

"I was almost eighteen weeks pregnant. I understood ultrasound to be standard." I didn't mean to sound like I was quizzing her.

"Is that it?" I motioned to the monitor behind her that seemed to glow in the darkened exam room. She spun around on her stool and deftly turned off the monitor button, leaving the machine to continue humming loudly from the built-in fan running to cool the large computer box. We were both quiet. The fan was all that existed between us. I started to cry and wiped my eyes with the back of my t-shirt sleeve. She rolled toward me and handed me one, two, three tissues, jutting her hand out toward me.

"I'm so sorry. I can talk to you about this because I'm a doctor. It would have been better coming from your OB, perhaps. This isn't what usually happens."

I stood in stunned silence as she went on. "This is resolvable. It's a simple D&E," she cleared her throat realizing that she had not chosen her words well. "I mean, it is the same thing you went through before, but it will most definitely be done with guided ultrasound, and you'll make a full recovery. You should be feeling better very soon."

I restrained myself from sharing my internal voice with her. *Feel better? How can I feel better when I have an urn of my baby's ashes at home that is so tiny a hummingbird would feel crowded in it? And now you're telling me that they butchered our baby?*

My mind flashed an after-image of what I had just seen on the screen before she turned it off—the alleged fragments of my wee baby where I had last seen him dancing about just a few months before. She began to make her exit strategy from the room after referring to my baby as "calcified parts," and she seemed to sense that her technical term had put her in deeper waters than her job description permitted. It was another blow, and I was sickened by the spiritual aspect of our baby not being retrieved "whole," of his body being further desecrated by having to be removed in two attempts. The ashes in my urn were not complete, and I knew they'd think me crazy if I asked for *the rest*. I steeled myself with the thought that I couldn't be the only woman to endure this complication. Dr. Parr's words the day of the amnio echoed in my head: "If we wait another week, I'll be getting out of my comfort zone."

My occasional arrhythmia had my heart pounding so hard I thought I might pass out. I wanted so much to confront Dr. Parr and scream at him.

How could he have done this to me? Why hadn't he been more aggressive in diagnosing the post-surgical pain? He became the enemy, the one onto whom I could safely pin some of my rage, as I struggled not to rage against God, Ben, or myself.

"I'm going to get our nurse who is good at explaining these things and can sit with you for a minute." She stood up slowly, using her hands to press against the top of her thighs.

These things? These things actually happen enough to have a person who's good at explaining them? I quietly wondered in my sarcastic inner voice.

"I wish I had the right thing to say, other than that you will feel better, and this will get better. Again, I'm so sorry for your loss, Jenny." She backed out of the dark room, turning up the lights on the dimmer switch, as if that might shock me back into composure—back to the face of a normal person, the polite person I always was.

I jerked my green stretchy pants down off the wall hook so hard that my underwear fell to the floor. I didn't care about them getting dirty. I didn't care about anything. I was pulling up my pants and gingerly trying to sit down sideways to put on my socks when the nurse to whom I'd been pawned off came in with my chart and a hand-held Palm Pilot fitted with a black rubber cover like a walkie-talkie. I knew why she was here. Her mission was scheduling.

"Hi, Mrs. Harper. Dr. Helsik sent me in to help you schedule your procedure in our next available time slot. Our obstetrical surgeries are done on Fridays."

"I know." I'd rarely answered anyone without including the words I'm sorry or thank you, but all I cared about was blowing my nose and collecting my purse and jacket so I could leave this place.

"How about we do this? I'll put you on the surgical schedule for next Friday with Dr. Parr, and then you talk to your husband and call Dr. Parr in the morning to make a plan of care."

"Okay. Thank you." I answered, barely hearing myself.

She handed me a blue folder with gold foil lettering, the same kind I received congratulating me on my pregnancy, with information about the hospital's birthing center, NICU, and maternal nutritional support resources. This time the blue folder was nearly empty, and she showed me the scheduling paper and pre-op instructions inside it.

"Yep. Got it. Thanks."

I paused to let her leave so I could be alone again in the room. I felt numb. I'd been in a room exactly like this in May when they'd told us we should end our baby's life. *It's the compassionate choice,* they had said. I'd spent much of my life in and out of medical centers, and for the first time I felt entitled to break the unspoken rules. I walked over to the ultrasound equipment that had been the bearer of the worst news of my life now twice. *They're my medical records anyway,* I thought as I listened carefully for noise in the hallway in the hopes I wouldn't be caught, and I pressed the red button on the computer monitor and paused as it changed to green.

Why are you doing this? I heard my mom whisper in my head. *Don't torture yourself.*

But I had to see it, to see what was left of him. *He was mine. He was not meant for medical waste.* I familiarized myself with the little pile of forgotten bones. I pressed my hand against the monitor over the cause of my ongoing pain and unresolved grief, now lit up in silence before me without any words needed from a medical provider.

"I'm sorry. I'm so sorry, little one."

The tears ran freely down my face, and I felt utterly alone in the world.

"God forgive me."

CHAPTER 9:

SECOND GOODBYE

(September 2000)

That September day came quickly, and Ben settled himself in the waiting room seat two rows over from where he sat in June for the first surgery. Thankfully, Dr. Parr agreed to allow a gastroenterologist to perform a partial colonoscopy under anesthesia at my request. I wanted to be sure that I was thoroughly examined so I could put the worries regarding any cancerous mass to bed forever. There had been a few conversations when I'd stepped outside of my shellshocked body to advocate for myself, but these flashes of assertiveness were fleeting. I didn't opt to change to a different OB-GYN because I took some comfort in the fact that Dr. Parr knew the situation and my medical history. Clarity of thought was like a tiny island that I swam to in between drowning. When each decision was made, I would stake myself to an imagined palm tree on this island of strength, only to find the sand dissolve beneath my feet until the dark and deep water swept me away again.

After another sleepless night, with a shallow smile on my face, I signed more consent forms for a repeat D&E, a colonoscopy, a hysteroscopy, and to be sure he did it right this time, an exploratory laparoscopy. After I checked in with the admission desk and got my bracelet for this second procedure, this medical do-over due to the incompetency of Dr. Parr, I found Ben reading a more up-to-date edition of the magazine he had nervously flipped through when we were last in this part of the hospital—the day we said goodbye to our baby. He seemed calm and not nervous at all. I knew what nervous felt like, but that's not what I was feeling. I sat down sideways, as had become my method for three months, and I held my purse out to him without words.

"What?" He looked annoyed to be interrupted from his reading.

"Can you take it now since they'll give it to you as soon as they take me up to the OR floor?"

"I don't need to take it now. Just wait."

As soon as he looked back down to his reading, I closed my eyes and tried to take a deep breath. So, this is what it felt like to be him, I imagined. To feel angry at the world and everyone all the time. I wanted to stand up and throw the purse at him, but stuffing it was more my style. I wanted to rip the magazine from his hands and raise my voice in public and proclaim the truth:

Guess why we're here, fellow waiting room patrons? While you may be here today for a tonsillectomy or a torn tendon, we're here to abort our son. Oh, wait. We already did that! In June. Same place, right here, same medical center, same doctors, same admitting staff, same parking lot. We're here to get on the roller coaster a second time, to see if they can do it right without butchering our baby again.

But instead of losing it, I took the anger, the horror, the fear of what I was about to face again, and I buried it. I pressed it down past my esophagus, past my lungs, down into my gut, somewhere underneath my diaphragm, and I swallowed hard to wash it down.

Just then I heard my name called, and I got up fast, securing the hospital gown behind me with my left hand, with no choice but to hand my purse to Ben. A nurse ushered us back through the double doors and down a long, white hall that was so bright I thought it was almost as blinding as an operating room. There were no pleasantries to exchange with the nurse, so we attended to the routine tasks of confirming my height, weight, and vitals. After asking me to verify my name and date of birth and my reason for being there, she escorted us to the elevator we awkwardly shared with another patient. I'd never been to a hospital where they had you walk around in a gaping gown all the way to the OR floor with virtually no privacy in what they called a "new concept" surgery center. I had other ideas about what I'd like to call it, but I had little mental resources left to be mad. The nerves were kicking in, and my stomach grumbled from fasting but also from the anxiety of another surgery. The nurse showed Ben to the waiting room off the elevator, as if he didn't know where to go.

"This is where you'll wait for her. Her admit number will show up on the TV monitor so you'll be able to track her progress."

"Yes, I know." He offered no pleasantries or a thank you, and he kissed me on the cheek, dropped my hand, and made his way back to our belongings. I felt something begin to tear in me, a kind of angry numbness, unable to process the out-of-body experience of aborting my beloved son now a second time.

Why is this happening, God? Is this punishment for us agreeing to end his life the first time? I thought, turning my back to leave Ben in the comfortable waiting room with free coffee.

"Okay, Jenny. Ready to go?" She was so nonchalant.

We weren't going for tea. *How could she be so upbeat?*

We didn't speak as I padded behind her in ugly grey hospital socks down the long and shiny hall. I followed her, obedient and wordless, until we were met by an orderly with black hair and tan arms who had a gurney waiting for me.

"Do you need help getting up?" he asked in a gentle whisper. He looked oddly familiar, so I blinked to make it go away.

"I can do it. Thanks." It was uncoordinated since I couldn't use all the strength of my legs, but I didn't want help from anyone.

I laid back on the gurney since sitting up would be awkward, and I knew how this was supposed to go. We waited there until another nurse came over, checked my ID bracelet, and put a warm blanket over me. It was the only comforting thing that pushed back the spreading nausea. I could feel the plastic of the pillow through the scratchy white pillowcase, and its familiarity triggered silent tears that ran down my cheek and hid themselves in my hair. The orderly wheeled me down the hall slowly, which was kind, and he was silent. I wondered if the silence between us was because he knew why I was there, or if he recognized me too. He maneuvered the gurney carefully around the last turn of the hallway to the operating room suites, and when the end of my bed hit the OR room door, I nearly cried out.

"Last time the gurney was too wide for the door and I had to walk myself in."

"I've got you. We've got it. No problem." I wanted to reach up for his hand and never let go. He was the first kind person I'd met that day.

Everything in the OR was exactly the same as it had been on that sunny day in June that was my darkest hour. I looked first at the clock to ensure it was right. I had refused to take the same surgery time as before. Something had to be different. The lights were so bright, and once on the operating table, I couldn't look at the operating room staff as directly as I had in June. The nurse anesthetist introduced herself while the anesthesiologist took my right hand and gave it a squeeze.

"We're gonna give you something right now to help you feel a little calmer, okay?" I wondered if he knew the situation. The IV was adjusted so quickly I didn't have time to tell him yes, and before I knew it the wall clock began to blur. I moved out of the pilot's seat and my body took over, no longer under my control.

The heavy feeling made me feel anxious, and I started to cry, hard.

"I can't. I can't."

"Hey, it's okay." It was the anesthesiologist again. "We gave you medication that should make you feel better in just a minute. You're okay, sweetheart."

Something inside my heart broke loose. I didn't know if it was God or my subconscious, but I couldn't process going through this exact same procedure again, a second time. Fighting the drug-induced sleep and wanting to get up and run, I saw Dr. Parr appear. He was gowned and tying his surgical mask.

Where's the ultrasound? I panicked and scanned the room with my eyes, unable to move my body. *I can't.*

"I want my baby!" I'd said it. I heard myself say it, but I was powerless to stop the words.

"I want my baby!"

The last thing I heard was the congestion of my breathing and the familiar beeping sounds of monitors around my head. The sweet sting of anesthesia ran up my arm, and the taste of cold liquid metal brought with it more panic, as I struggled to get one last voluntary deep breath. Fighting the anesthesia made it worse, and I felt suffocated as the mask was pressed softly over my nose. It made an inescapable seal, and I breathed in the cool oxygen until the lights changed from white hot pain to blackness.

CHAPTER 10

FIRSTS

(2001)

My son Nathaniel would have celebrated his first birthday on November 11, 2001. Instead of frosting cupcakes and organizing a family party with my nearly four-year-old daughter running around excitedly wanting to help me blow up balloons, Ben and I were in the middle of a divorce and I was longing for my baby boy. I promised myself I would do something special on his birthday starting that day and ever year thereafter. The company I worked for recognized the eleventh of November, Veterans Day as a paid holiday. I was able to stay home that morning with Lily and plan something special for myself, but also do something with a community focus to help someone else. I had permission to visit the local nursing home where there were many residents who did not have family to visit regularly. I dressed Lily in a striped fall dress, tights and coat, and she stepped into her red rain boots at the door as we gathered our things. Her boots were a wardrobe staple she donned daily, like other children of the Pacific Northwest—children I felt sure would all be doomed to fallen arches. We set out with toddler car snacks, washed hands and open hearts, hoping to bless others.

When we arrived at the nursing home, we learned that the lady we were assigned for the afternoon was in her late 80s, and after she let us into her apartment, she soon told us that she was the woman who'd inspired the comic strip *Blondie*. Though the visit was intended to be short, we chatted effortlessly for two hours. Her wonderful stories had me pinned to her upholstered chair, listening closely in fascination as Lily played on the floor next to me with some quiet toys from the little backpack I had prepared for her. A tin of cookies and an African violet no longer seemed an adequate gift for this gracious lady who laughed and smiled at the antics and chatter of my preschooler. She showed us a wonderful scrapbook of black and white photos, neatly held by yellowing photo corners. She wasn't wearing makeup, but her white hair was recently set and tidy. Lily ate a sandwich baggie of goldfish and finished her juice box while we visited and was starting to quietly whine that she was hungry. I gathered up our things and hugged the beautiful woman tightly, bending down into her chair. She smelled like soap and baby wipes and old perfume, and it was wonderful. She called Lily over to say goodbye, but, too shy to hug, Lily handed her a picture she'd been coloring on the floor. It was hard to leave her, as I feared I would not visit again when life returned to its furious pace, but it had been a special visit for all of us.

Once in the car, I cranked the heater knob to max and the compressor of our old Subaru rattled in time with the cold pistons of the laboring engine.

"Can I get a Happy Meal, Mama?

I wasn't a fan of fast food, especially McDonald's, but I made my peace with occasionally indulging Lily after her intermittent toddler hunger strikes. She ate like a bird, but if it was a cheeseburger, she ate the whole patty, and I was just happy she ate. It was a different kind of day, a special day, and if a Happy Meal made her happy, so be it.

"If you eat your cheeseburger first before opening the toy, we can go. Should we eat McDonald's at the park?" I looked in my rearview mirror to see she had her blanket snuggled up by her face, signaling she would be ready for a long nap after lunch and playtime.

"Can I play on the slides too?"

"It's a little cold and windy, bunny, but let's eat in the car, and if it's warm enough you can play until 12:45 and then it's home for nap, okay?" I glanced back again to see her nodding her head up and down in agreement with her thumb in her mouth. I was glad I'd had her use the potty and wash hands before we left the nursing home. Her thumb was my greatest frustration in germ management and my greatest blessing as a parent, as she was an incredible self-soother and a sound sleeper.

"Okay, Mama," and back in went the thumb as I turned around in a cul-de-sac and we headed toward McDonald's, the only drive-through around for twenty miles.

The park was nearly empty this late in the year except for a few bundled tots running from tire swing to sand box, donning knit caps and their own rubber boots in red and other primary colors. After we parked, Lily crawled into the front seat next to me and began telling me her version of tales about the lady with the white hair.

"Why couldn't we eat the cookies we brought to the lady?" she asked through bites of hamburger bun.

"The cookies were a present from us to her. We don't eat a present that we give to someone else."

I knew the one who'd received a gift today had been me, and I knew I would remember the beautiful lady forever. The details of that first November anniversary in 2001 were not only sketched in pencil but were covered with thick blobs of oil paint—permanently rendered in my mind in vivid 3D.

Over the years, the eleventh of November came to signal a day off from work to reflect and do something positive and kind for myself and others. I learned that Veterans Day is called "Remembrance Day" in Canada, and I was struck by the beauty of what that meant for me and my own remembering heart. Some years Lily would spend Veterans Day with her dad, and while I missed her, it afforded me the freedom to do some self-care. One year I got a pedicure and drove around taking a self-guided tour of the fall leaves around the county as I listened to songs that made me think of my baby boy. No anniversary was complete without a visit to the park where I had taken Lily for McDonald's on that first anniversary, and the same park where I donated a brick paver toward the construction of a new playground in 2001, which seemed a simple and fitting memorial. The books I'd read in an effort to make the grief go away all spoke of memorializing your unborn child in some way. The paver gave me a place to go every November to remember my son, because like many women who terminate a pregnancy, I had no gravesite to visit, and there was no stone or marker or cemetery. This paver gave me a place to go where I could briefly kneel down and brush away the dirt and sand to see the words that made my baby real. I didn't want my daughter to think that I had a ghost in my life, and I never spoke of it to her until she was old enough to understand that she had a baby brother in heaven. Parents who have suffered a loss can sometimes be overprotective of other children in a dysfunctional way. I have frequently said, "Lily is the spring in my step and the catch in my throat." It seemed fitting that the paver at the park read, "Angels on earth and in heaven. Lily & Natty 2000."

A splash pad was later added to the park's play area where Lily and I had fun passing afternoons with her cousin and her friends. It was a safe place for her to ride her bike around sections of the flat walking path that encircled the 90-acre park. My memories here were safe and happy.

One particular weekend, I was at a loss for an activity for Lily. There were intense legal proceedings going on related to Ben and I divorcing, and she was struggling with separation anxiety. We took a picnic blanket and a simple lunch to the park where there happened to be an English horseback riding competition featuring beautiful show horses that were scheduled to be jumping that afternoon. I was thrilled at the prospect of free entertainment and the opportunity to watch the controlled chaos of the muscles of the beautifully braided horses in action. My little girl had never sat frozen and silent for such a long period of time as she did that afternoon. Lily was completely enraptured by the horses. I had no idea then that my daughter would later become an accomplished equestrian and go on to ride in this same prestigious show.

CHAPTER 11:

ANGRY

(June 2000)

I opened the greeting card inside the lavender envelope, noting that it was a Hallmark brand.

"Nice," I said out loud, not meaning to sound sarcastic.

I was relieved and almost thankful it was not another Christian card that would contain a Bible verse that might have been comforting years from now, I didn't know. This week, Bible verses were sitting about as well as a spicy burrito at midnight. *Was I angry at God?* I didn't care. It was too exhausting to think about. Up all night with my toddler who'd been coughing, I felt the heaviness of an oncoming cold descending into my chest. It was June— "Juneuary" as we called it in the Pacific Northwest—where it could rain the entire month of June if Seattle found it amusing. Lily was perpetually sick regardless of my best efforts, especially in the winter, and I was hoping to get a break now that summer was just around the corner. I was angry about the cold—angry about everything right now.

I knew what had set me off on the wrong foot this morning, and it wasn't sleep deprivation from a coughing toddler. It was a yellow shirt that had fallen on my head from the top shelf of our closet with a heap of other folded sweatshirts. I forced myself to go back to fold the pile of tumbled sweatshirts, recalling how the yellow shirt had come to be up in the corner of the closet. When the doctors had given us the life-changing news about our son that day, we'd come home from the hospital to my parent's innocent questions asking what was wrong with the baby. I'd been angry at the injustice of feeling pregnant and happy that morning only to have it taken away in a high-rise ultrasound room that same afternoon. If our baby was going to die, I didn't want to be pregnant anymore, maybe not ever again. I remembered how I'd ripped the yellow shirt off my body, a button flying off in my fury. As I knelt to pick it up from the closet floor, I remembered how it had felt like alligator skin that day, betraying me against my arms. In my anger, I'd thrown it into the farthest corner of the closet shelf, as if filing it away, unable to deal with the grief it represented. I didn't want anyone to wear it. It held the alcohol vapors of hospital smell in its folds, and its cheerful color boasted in contrast to the storm clouds forming over our home.

I folded one sweatshirt, then another, but I left the offending maternity shirt where it lay on the closet floor. I slid down the wall to sit on the carpet as if to join it. I picked it up and began angrily wringing the shirt as if to strangle it for falling down on me, until my anger was replaced with sobs. I hugged the shirt to my chest between my knees and my breasts that were still painful from the postpartum hormone changes for which no one had prepared me.

From where I sat on the closet floor, I could see the bathroom, and another memory from that fateful day came over me like a flashbulb. I saw my pregnant self awkwardly spread out on the cold vinyl floor sorting through plastic bins, unfazed by Ben's sudden appearance in the bathroom doorway.

"What are you doing?" he asked me with a warble in his throat.

"I can't find my vitamins. They were just here this morning. I always keep them under the sink right in front, and I didn't take them this morning because I wasn't supposed to eat, and I have to take them now!"

The tears were close to coming, but I didn't dare cry in front of him, especially over vitamins.

"That's ridiculous! Did you hear what they said today? The baby's not okay."

I closed my eyes and tuned out his familiar mocking tone in an attempt to grab hold of the locomotive I heard in my head. It was roaring and grating on steel, and I needed to run and catch up to the train, to escape him, to escape this—to catch a rusty metal hook of it and to let it drag me along like the broken rag doll I was becoming.

"We're probably not going to keep the baby. Why on earth would you take vitamins now?" His voice sounded like sandpaper, and the helplessness I felt turned inward to silent anger that rose up into my esophagus with burning acid.

Answering him was not an option, so I swallowed hard. *How could he say that? We hadn't made any real decisions, but he was talking about our baby as if he was already gone. He—a boy. We were having a boy. Couldn't he just let me have that for a few hours, a few days?* Reaching up from the floor to grab the white porcelain sink, I awkwardly pulled myself up.

"I have to take my vitamins. Of course it still matters! We haven't made a decision. I'm still pregnant, and I'm still his mom."

He stepped toward me throwing an arm out to sloppily drape it around my neck in what I hoped would be compassion, a sideways hug, anything.

"Don't worry about it. There's a lot to worry about right now and that hardly seems important. You'll drive yourself crazy over things like that."

"I have to take my vitamins until the last day, even if we go forward with their recommendations. We haven't decided. We haven't decided." I held my breath waiting for a retaliatory comeback.

Ben was already walking away, taking care to slam the door on the way out of our bedroom. I was shaking from the cold of wearing only a maternity bra and leggings mixed with the adrenaline of our discord. It was always best to let him have the last word. I reached for one of his oversized flannel shirts, but it smelled like sawdust, and I quickly threw it in the hamper.

I couldn't face putting on another maternity shirt from my dresser. I knew there was an obstinate yellow button that had landed there, and I didn't want it looking up at me with holes like little mocking eyes. I wiped my nose on my sweatshirt sleeve and looked up at my hanging clothes. There was a maternity sweater that looked soft, but still had the tags on it. It was for next month when I'd be bigger, but at least it would cover the baby bump and not pull against my middle. There was nothing to hang on to in that cold bedroom, not even my husband, and the department store smell was a welcome relief from flashbacks of the hospital. From where I stood in the closet, I could see the book *What to Expect When You're Expecting* just under the corner of our bed. The cover was worn, though it was purchased new for this, our second pregnancy. I had given away my first copy to another expecting mom. A flash of anger took hold of me as I threw it against the wall. I'd thrown a few things in my life, but never a book. Books were to be revered and cared for, a value on which Ben and I both agreed, but these days there was a first time for everything.

The lingering mess in the closet pulled me back to the present and the comforting monotony of folding the sweatshirts that had triggered the flashbacks. The velvet voice of my congested toddler startled me as she appeared in the closet door, making it easy to abandon my memories surrounding the yellow shirt.

"Why are you in the closet, Mama?"

"Oh, I was just folding some sweatshirts that fell down on Mama's head. Can you believe that?"

She was giggling with a juice box straw in her mouth. It struck me that someday when she was much older, I might tell her a little more about her baby brother in heaven. But for now, taking care of her cough and nurturing that giggle was not only my sanity, but the most perfect thing in the world.

CHAPTER 12:

SALVATION

(Fall 2000)

My emerging tendency toward double-mindedness faced off like a storm front where cold air and warm air met at a convergence zone. I presented my front to the world in one way, but underneath a storm was raging. A mid-life crisis was moving in a decade too early and right at the crossroads before finding my faith. I wasn't ready to seek God until I was mature enough to stand up against the cold front that pushed hard into me each time I planned to go to church. This cold front was Ben's repetitive mocking of what he said was weakness—the need to seek something larger than myself. At church, I felt the warm air envelop me and my daughter the instant we walked through the door, where for two hours I left the chill of my marriage behind me. My return to church just months before the story of our son unfolded was no coincidence. It wasn't until I reached the bottom of the brokenness of my abortion that I began to hunger for understanding of God's true and gentle character. In my head I knew that Jesus had been with me through both of my life-changing surgeries, but I was ready to learn about how I could pursue a meaningful relationship with God the Son.

At church, I felt welcomed and comfortable, and I quickly met new people, enjoyed the worship and singing, listened intently to the message from the pastor, and wrote down upcoming social events. I had worked through the social handicapping of my childhood that came with not being one of the parish families—the only non-Catholic kid in my school. I had embraced Catholicism out of a genuine interest in knowing God, but as an adult, I found that church became less anxiety-provoking and more like a place of comfort. When the pastor spoke of salvation, I was unsure of all the steps that would be required of me, but in spite of Ben's protestations, when Lily wasn't sick, I'd pack her up and I kept going to church. These early steps of recovering my faith gave me a safe place in which to begin to recover.

One Sunday I heard a sermon that suggested God knew exactly the number of days marked out for every child, which meant that He knew all about Nathaniel's life before He put him in my womb. He knew the decision my husband and I would make long before we did, and none of the tragic components of our story were a surprise to Him. The storm fronts in my life were teaching me that asking "why" didn't get me anywhere but smack dab in the middle of despair. As I began to reframe life's difficult questions with, "how" my empty glass began to fill again. I listened to new church friends ask questions like, "How can we use trials to glorify God?" or, "How can we use our testimony to help other people?" I had no idea how my abortion trauma could possibly be used to help others grow deeper in faith, but each time I made it to church, my perspective began to expand beyond the four walls of our increasingly tense home.

The first night after the abortion I couldn't sleep. In between staring at the porch light on the back deck through swollen eyes, crying quietly so as not to wake Ben, I got up, exasperated. The only place to go was the living room, which offered a couch and the warmth of our sleeping cats. The physical and emotional pain were warring with exhaustion, and I felt all I could do was pace. When the pain became too great, I'd cautiously lie down on the couch. The only Bible I owned, newly found for church, was on top of some fishing magazines on our dated oak coffee table. It was just sitting there, asking nothing of me. The heaviness I felt made me long for the sting of an IV, something that would take me out of my body and carry me off to a place of escape. My well-toned bootstrap muscles of self-reliance were too fatigued to pull myself up on my own. I stared at the Bible, shivering for what felt like an hour. Our grey tabby cat stood up from where he lay on my feet and stretched tall like a Halloween cat, leaving the warmth of his sister. I watched him jump down and creep silently over the transition from the carpet to the kitchen vinyl, where he stopped to take a long drink. The sound of him lapping water from his dish revived me enough to push up against the arm of the couch until I was sitting, balancing my weight on my left hip. I picked up the Bible in total despair and flipped it to a random page, hoping it would somehow speak to me. In spite of the pain and chills, as I cried quietly, I found myself in Psalm 91.

> "He will cover you with his feathers,
> and under his wings you will find refuge;
> his faithfulness will be your shield and rampart.
> You will not fear the terror of night,
> nor the arrow that flies by day,
> nor the pestilence that stalks in the darkness,
> nor the plague that destroys at midday."

(Psalm 91:4-6)

I held the Bible to my chest, and I sobbed, unprotected and vulnerable under a flimsy blue knit blanket. In the living room, lit only by a solitary floor lamp, I cried out to God with no more elegance than the whispered words, *Help me.*

My midlife crisis wasn't like the kind on a TV commercial where a fifty-year-old guy impulsively buys a Harley-Davidson motorcycle to reconnect with his youth, to fight against the aging process, or maybe simply because he can finally afford it. I had faced trials with youth and energy reserves on my side, and I had done it on my own, until the loss of my baby. It was the defining moment, the crossroad when my life turned in a different direction and finally toward the cross. God was profoundly merciful to help me reach out to Him just in time. My life had become a transitional season of polarized bookends that sharply contrasted my emerging faith against the impending chaos of divorce proceedings.

Several surgeries stacked up in the first years after my abortion, and it was humiliating to learn that I often woke up in the recovery room involuntarily crying and calling out for my baby. I kept a tight lid on my public self, but I was mortified that the pain I kept pushed down would keep leaking out under anesthesia. Experiencing both D&E surgeries close together, coupled with infections, led to a condition called irritable uterus. I changed to a compassionate and outgoing female OB-GYN, and she began her plan of care with an ultrasound to ensure things had finally returned to a pre-pregnancy state. She was kind, and she shared a few printed pictures from the ultrasound with me at my follow-up visit. She pointed out a white line through the middle of my uterus, and explained that it was likely scar tissue, created by calcifications. Learning about this finding was not a positive thing physically, but emotionally it was validating to see that the scars I carried in my heart also existed physically in my body. It offered a valid explanation for the lingering pain and discomfort that caused me to question if it was only in my head. I was so relieved that when she left the room, I got dressed and rested for a minute on the cold Formica bench to let the feelings come with abandon. Someone finally understood that the physical damage of my abortion was not only emotionally credible but was medically validated.

My early mid-life crisis was a series of life-changing trials. The medical complications were devastating, and the end of our son's life coincided with the end of our marriage. The tragic loss of our baby was the final blow, but the marriage was already in tatters. The circumstances of Nathaniel's life were not responsible for the outcome of my relationship with Ben, but the timing was more than our troubled marriage could carry. God went before me to lay a foundation of new friends and support through a church family He knew I would need, and He placed a Bible out on a coffee table in the darkest of nights. Sometimes it is in the deepest valleys that we are forced to search for light, and as my son's life came to a close, a new life of salvation was opening for me.

CHAPTER 13:

SHACKLED

(2006)

My early years as a Christian, divorced and dating, and regularly attending church on Sundays were busy and complicated. I continued to struggle with pride, self-reliance, and maintaining the approval of others. In spite of the daily joys of being a mom, enjoying the novelty of singlehood and the accolades found in an advancing career, feelings of shame and self-loathing of my physical body rarely left me.

The God I knew from childhood was demanding, vengeful, unforgiving, and He was measuring my performance more than anyone else. The early years of my return to church confirmed my thoughts that the God of the Old Testament was likely still merciless, demanding, and full of wrath.

One Tuesday night as I set up coffee service before Bible study, I was rushing to finish my homework before the ladies arrived. I had just written out the words of (1 John 1:9) which states, "If we confess our sins, he is faithful and just and will forgive us our sins and purify us from all unrighteousness." I stared out the windows of our church fellowship hall as the rain beat mercilessly against the concrete building, and I meditated on the word *confess*. My few acts of confession before being found out by Sister Zip Zip of my childhood had given me a curious glimpse into a world of secrecy and shame. My mind drifted back to the few confessional experiences I participated in before I was outed as a non-Catholic. I found myself once again on the familiar wooden pews, feeling cold under my uniform skirt and with a ball of anxiety forming in my stomach. I was too young to have a long list of sins from which to choose at confession, and I listened to the kids around me talking about the sins they planned to share with Father Bruce.

"What are you gonna say to him?" I whispered to Maggie who sat in front of me.

"I stole my brother's homework, so he'd get in trouble for not doing it," she laughed through her braces when she turned around to answer me.

"I talked back to my dad at the dinner table last Tuesday," Ellie chimed in.

I didn't have any siblings I could draw from in order to conjure up a juicy story to confess to Father Bruce. Even then, I suspected I was a good kid, and I searched my heart and mind for something confession worthy.

"What are *you* telling him?" I asked Beth who sat to my left, her black patent leather shoes dangling over the edge of the pew, too short to touch the ground.

"Um, well, yesterday I thought about how I was so mad at my mom for making me do the dishes again."

"How's that bad?" I interrupted her.

"Well, it was wrong for me to be mad at her." Jason pulled at the ribbon in her hair, and she spun around to grab for his hand.

"We can't be mad at anybody?" I asked, not the least bit interested in Jason after Beth's revelation.

"No, dummy. I had bad thoughts. You know, *bad* thoughts."

"Thoughts?" I asked with furrowed eyebrows, crinkling up my nose.

She was fixing her ribbon back into a bow when our teacher gestured to her to put her hands back in her lap.

"We can confess our thoughts?"

"Of course," she chided me. "There's lots to confess! It can be a mortal sin, or it can be like eating too much candy." She seemed so sure of her explanation.

She resumed swinging her legs, and I became lost in swirling thoughts.

Back in the present chill of the church hall where I sat waiting for the ladies to arrive for Bible study, I stood up to welcome my first visitor and help her get some coffee.

My impressions of the Sacrament of Reconciliation might have been different if I'd received a fully sanctioned course of Catholic education, but I was forever changed by the impression made on my immature and innocent mind that day. The words *"I'm sorry"* became part of my daily vocabulary, and I committed to regularly searching my mind and heart for any transgressions I could find. I never wanted to find myself in line for confession again without something scandalous to get off my chest.

On a particularly memorable business trip to Florida in 2006, I plopped down in my fiercely guarded aisle seat on the plane and held my purse to my chest, politely waiting to fasten my seatbelt until the balance of my row was filled. A tan man in a coral linen shirt eased past me with a polite, "Excuse me," and deftly molded himself into the window seat. The plane was nearly full, and I began to get excited that perhaps I wouldn't have a neighbor in the middle seat next to me and my personal bubble could be preserved. The luggage bin flew open above me, and I looked up to find a skeletal woman in a black business suit wrestling with her laptop bag in growing frustration. The flight attendant motioned to her with a nonverbal pantomime, as if to say, "That's not gonna work." I fished around in my purse for the fresh pack of six-dollar airport Doublemint gum I needed for my customary take off ritual, when something hard and heavy landed squarely across the top of my head.

"Ow!" I squeaked, trying to be as quiet as possible, but the pain was sharp and instant.

"Oh no! Are you okay?" My coral-shirted neighbor reached over to touch my forearm.

"Um. Sure. I think so." I couldn't finish because little silver flecks danced around the corners of my eyes when I looked up to ensure no one was watching.

"Hey, ma'am!" Mr. Coral Shirt called out to the black-suited pencil lady, startling me as I tucked my hair behind my ears.

The lady in black was trying to force her laptop bag into the overhead bin across from our row, but my handsome window seat knight wasn't having it.

"Seriously? You dropped your luggage on this lady's head!"

"It's okay," I stammered before pencil lady could whisper under her breath and resume shoving her bag into an impossible space.

"I'm fine. I'm sorry." I looked at him sheepishly.

"The nerve of some people!" He was fired up, and it felt unexpected and nice to have him stand up for me.

"Should I have the flight attendant get you some ice for your head?"

"Oh, no. Thank you. Thank you for being so kind."

In my hotel room later that night when I told the tale to Garrett, who was then my boyfriend, he was incredulous.

"You told her you were sorry? She should have apologized to you!"

I regularly caught myself apologizing while navigating something as simple as the grocery store. If someone hit my cart, I was quick to say "I'm sorry," like it was an involuntary reflex. Family and friends teased me about it, but my attempts to replace the word *sorry* with anything else proved fruitless. I came to realize that chronic apologizing was a distant cousin to my longtime battle with the communion of my past, where my subconscious mind constantly reminded me of my unworthiness as I recited, "Lord, I'm not worthy to receive You, but only say the word and I shall be healed."

For a lifetime I had misinterpreted this prayer as shame over my life, rather than the true intention.

The day the lady dropped the twenty-five-pound laptop bag on my head, my instinct was to say "I'm sorry," as an outward assertion of my unworthiness. Whenever I apologized unnecessarily, I wished I could shake the shoulders of a younger me. I wanted to ask myself why I'd felt it necessary to apologize to the callous woman who dropped the luggage on my head, as if to tell her I was sorry to be sitting in that particular seat on that particular day, giving her laptop a soft place to fall. Sometimes the little things in life were what opened me up to learn the big lessons—dysfunctional patterns I had held in my craw since childhood. It was both painful and liberating to see where I had been shackled.

CHAPTER 14:

WOUNDS

(2008)

It is often said that it's the truth that sets us free, but for many abortion survivors, the truth is impossible to speak. I spent a lot of my life putting lipstick on situations that warranted nothing more than a broom and a dustpan. I excelled at making light of bad situations, but it took a long time to learn that lipstick doesn't fix everything, and I was denying and stuffing complex and life-changing pain. Now, after two decades to think about my abortion decision, the image that often comes to mind is of the human heart, made up of four chambers and an outer covering called the pericardium. When I analyzed the thought process I went through when faced with a medically advised abortion, I later realized that I made the decision quickly, thinking I had fully engaged my heart, only to find out later that there was delayed processing that caught up to me. I followed the advice of medical providers who would never have to live with the natural consequences of my decision. I made the heartbreaking choice to terminate in shock, disbelief, and anxiety, in the outer anatomy of my heart—the pericardium. I did not filter my decision through the life-giving chambers of my heart nor through the eyes of my Creator by communing with Him in prayer. I did not come to full faith in Christ until March of 2001, after my son was gone. It took years to fully process the profound regret I felt, wishing I had taken more time to sit with and better understand the long-term consequences of abortion.

Other than online support groups where I searched for other parents who opted for medical termination, no one other than our family knew the circumstances surrounding our pregnancy loss. Comparisons existed inside my head that were quick and piercing. A mom would confide in me, "We had two miscarriages before getting pregnant with our second baby." Immediately, I would think to myself, *I'm so sad for her*, but my next thought would be, *I wish that was how I lost my baby*. As immature as it felt to think this, it was an automatic and private way of expressing what I felt every day—regret. When a new friend at church told me they were praying for a miracle for a family whose baby was diagnosed with Down Syndrome, I felt compassion, and I earnestly prayed for them, but my heart ached with simultaneous empathy and agony as I thought, *See…they're waiting it out to see if their baby might be healed. I didn't wait.*

One afternoon as I rounded the smoothly banked corner of a rural country highway, I received a phone call from a client who had become a close friend. She and her husband had just received the worst news of their lives that their first baby, a girl, had been diagnosed with mosaic trisomy 16, and they'd been advised to terminate the pregnancy. She talked in shallow breaths and gulps as she relayed the story to me. I pulled my car over into the parking lot of a local air conditioning company, took a few deep breaths with her, and we cried together. The next two nights left me feeling anxious and unable to sleep, as I imagined what was playing out over at their house. I knew they were probably not sleeping either and were wrestling with what they should do. She and her husband had the weekend to do research and agonize over their decision, and Monday when I called to check on her, she updated me that they'd decided to go forward with the pregnancy.

"We want her no matter what," she said with clear resolution.

I was so relieved for them, and I cried in joy with her on the phone as I let her know that I'd stand by her as a friend to support her no matter what life dealt them. When their daughter was born prematurely, weighing two pounds four ounces, I had the honor of holding her in the NICU. I sat in awe watching their tiny angel fight hard to survive amidst a feeding tube, supplemental oxygen, and IVs, with surgical tape covering more than half of this shockingly small pink doll. She seemed so fragile and yet she was so strong. Diagnostic genetic tests following her birth confirmed that the devastating birth defect was miraculously contained to the placenta. Their powerful testimony is one of pure hope, faith, and love. Watching her grow and thrive, fully overcoming a devastating diagnosis, is inspirational, and it is an honor to know such a miraculous child. To look at pictures of this beautiful young lady, no one could detect that she faced the impossible. When I reflect on the story of this family's victory, my eyes water over, and I wonder…if we had said we wanted Nathaniel "no matter what," whether he might have had a chance to be a miracle, too. It was the first day I began to process the painful reality of how desperately I still wanted my baby, damaged or not.

Trauma brings out the worst and the best in people, and my friend and her family powerfully illustrated human hearts at their best, carrying on with demonstrable courage. While I've been told I'm a friend who can be counted on, a friend who is truly empathetic, I was not a superhero. The impossible choice we made in 2000 put me in touch with the back-office side of myself, the back side of my ribbon, too unraveled to be double-faced—part of me I didn't know existed until I was broken. My shame and self-loathing caused me to compare myself to our mama dog rejecting her runt puppy. It was self-condemnation I felt I deserved. The dark side of me secretly wished to go back in time and lose my baby through the involuntary experience of miscarriage, which I imagined would have let me off the hook. After the abortion, there were nights when I heard the cruelest whisper pass over me in the darkest hour of the night, rousing me awake to say, *You are a murderer.*

It was a thought that could only come from an unmistakable enemy who was the prince of accusation. I never thought condemnation over anyone else, especially not a vulnerable and grieving woman. I had compassion for every woman in the world who had an abortion yet had no compassion for myself. I just knew that what we had done, what I had done, was wrong.

It was wrong for me. It was wrong for my emerging faith. It was wrong for me to say I was pro-choice, and it was wrong for me to say I was pro-life. Everything about it reeked of regret. It smelled because it was a wound, a wound that was so deep, so infected, in such an awkward place that I couldn't lance it myself. There wasn't an obvious incision that could be cleaned and dressed and monitored for infection. The scalpel of my shame created wounds that cut deep places in my heart and in my soul, leaving an indelible mark. I couldn't see that the wounding had formed scar tissue so deep and so corded that it created a wall obstructing not just my physical and emotional healing but my spiritual growth. I left the hospital that fateful day in 2000 with antibiotics, pain meds, and ice packs, but I also left a part of myself behind forever. I was changed, and it was not for the better. I could rationalize it away, but my body was telling me something vastly different.

When a wound scabs over on the outside, there can still be infection at the core. The initial pain of cleaning and dressing a wound is much easier to endure than the pain of a festering injury. Wounds are to be dealt with expeditiously and not ignored, kept clean and dry, lightly covered and out of extended periods of darkness. Light is healing for wounds—sunshine, heat lamps, lasers, and so many other healing therapies—but darkness fosters the growth of bacteria and mold and fungus. I had the kind of wound that was to remain unspoken, untended, without light and without air. I couldn't tell anyone the truth of how I'd come by this wound, let alone wear it on the outside where the light of truth might have accelerated the healing. My wound grew in direct correlation to the secret urn of ashes I first hid in a sock drawer, then in a shoe box, and later in a larger wooden box. The wound grew into a stronghold in my life, festering time and again until it outgrew any neat and tidy packaging I could arrange for it. Any nurse can tell you that infection stinks. I kept a polished exterior, clean and tidy, with natural makeup and appropriate clothing, but I was living a lie, hiding my self-loathing just under the surface. I may have been unleashed from the responsibility of a poor fetal prognosis, but on that day, I became shackled to shame.

I kept my feelings of shame outwardly hidden, but they festered on the inside. Life's distractions gave me a tidy excuse to avoid dealing with them. I had a tsunami of an endless divorce to deal with, a child who was often sick, and a job that ran at a furious pace. There was no time to cry or be "inappropriate." There was no time to be weak. There was no time to be anything other than a model employee and a good mother. I was insulated by an overbooked schedule that kept me distracted from night to night. I was delighted to be a mother to a precocious and sensitive little girl who made the hard work of daily life sparkle with joy and promise.

CHAPTER 15:

ASHES

(2009)

About nine years into my post-abortion journey, I began to contemplate what to do with the little urn of ashes, because it felt morbid to keep the urn forever. I occasionally had the courage to go the urn, to untie the little string around the top of the crimson velvet bag, to take it out and feel its metallic cold pull the heat from my hand. I always hit a wall that felt awkward and uncomfortable. Intentionally touching it was weird. I didn't want to be weird, so I put it away. I was dancing cautiously along a new layer of the complex onion of grief but touching the urn of ashes made my eyes water. Back into the velvet bag went the urn, put away, done.

The placement of the little paver at the park in 2001 had rendered it a sacred place for me. The paver created a reason for the park to become an acceptable memorial, a place where I could acknowledge that my baby was real. Every year without exception I went to the park on the eleventh of November to see the paver and to take a walk around the scenic and serene pond. One year when I visited the park in November, the memorial paver was gone, pulled up and replaced with new turf for the play structure. It had been ripped up and likely thrown into the back of a dump truck, and I too felt as if something had been ripped away from me, leaving me feeling empty.

A within-town move disrupted the box of Nathaniel's things triggering a significant grief episode that left me crying on the floor of my closet for at least an hour, perhaps longer. It was the urn of ashes nestled inside the box that provided simultaneous security and anxiety, and I began to wonder if it would be best to scatter his ashes, and if that might help me begin to let go. With the gentle encouragement of my husband, Garrett, I decided to release the ashes, and there was no need to muse over where to do it. The pond, his pond, seemed the perfect location.

My ninth November walk along the path to the pond felt like an eternity as I clutched the urn inside my coat pocket. I wasn't wearing gloves, wanting to somehow feel closer to him, to let the warmth of my mother's hand radiate inside to ashes that I knew no longer held his spirit. I ran my index finger back and forth over the shiny metal secret in my pocket, back and forth over the rim of the lid until it began to hurt. I wanted to remember the pain of that day, and I didn't want an occasional park visitor or runner to catch on to what I was about to do. Always one to fill silence with words, sitting still was one of the most difficult tasks for me, let alone sitting on the bench of the pond's gazebo in extended prayer time. The anxiety of finality left me with nothing else to do but talk silently in my head with Jesus, and I had given Him a special invitation to be my guest that day and to walk this out with me. How I wished that God would audibly speak. If only He would answer my questions by email—even a short text would do. I was relieved no one could hear my private thoughts.

Are You there, God?

Why can't I hear You?

Why can't I feel You?

As I steeled myself to face scattering the ashes I had perhaps held too tightly, a mother and her preschooler in a smart navy jacket headed my way riding a red tricycle, just like the trike I rode around the rough aggregate patio of my childhood home. It was the same model I bought for my daughter. An image of her riding it when she was four played behind my eyes as I looked at this little boy and his mother. I felt happy, thankful, and sad all mixed up like a blended drink. Seeing boys who were close to the age Nathaniel should have been or boys who looked like I imagined he would look stung me. With my free hand, I quickly wiped away a rogue tear and mustered my best smile for them as they passed. With the intrusion of the outside world, I had lost my nerve. I was cold but determined to try prayer again. After all, I only came out here once a year, and things needed to go a certain way, the way I had imagined. I closed my eyes again but did not bow my head.

I got up and walked gingerly on top of the wet leaves leading to the pond, where the ducks played in seemingly irreverent little groups, making the pond feel unworthy to receive my son. The mossy patches between the shiny leaves became Technicolor under the sun's warmth. I had never seen such beautiful foliage before, and I made a mental note to take some leaves home. Then it hit me, and I stopped. I was no longer walking on maple and cottonwood leaves with their traditional shapes, many of them the size of my face. My path was lined with leaves shaped just like hearts.

What are these? What kind of tree has heart-shaped leaves? I searched my mind for logical answers.

We do evergreen here, I thought with a touch of cynicism.

I tucked my awkward laugh back into the warmth of my scarf as if to ensure that no one would hear the thoughts in my head. I knelt down to pick up one of the heart-shaped leaves and was overcome. My loneliness was gone. My long-held anger at God for the events that surrounded my baby's return to heaven began to thaw, and I felt the presence of my friend Jesus.

Nathaniel. I heard my baby's name in my head, whispered in my own voice. In that moment I felt a strong inclination to change the spelling of his name to Nathanael, as it was spelled in the Bible. There was no one to ask for permission to change his name, no relationship intact to ask Ben if he was okay with it. There was no obituary or official marker in a cemetery and there was no medical record of his personhood other than an operative report. At the medical institution where his life was ended, he was simply referred to as "POC Harper," products of conception.

I'm giving him back to You, Lord. You know how sorry I am. Today I give Nathaniel back to You, renaming him like Nathanael in the Bible, to honor in some small way how faithful You've been to me, Jesus. Thank You. Amen

I dropped the urn back into my pocket to begin gathering the largest and most colorful of the accidental hearts that lined my path. It was as if some kind of ethereal flower girl had come before me to sprinkle these along the way. I let the tears come, and it felt as though I was held.

Park visitors had all but vanished. The noisy ducks seemed to settle themselves. As I prayed, the silence became noticeable, almost loud. There were no planes overhead. It was as if even the songbirds gave pause. How I longed for the sound of the breeze in the trees that had visited me just hours after leaving the hospital with empty arms. I clung to the wish that day that it might be my baby saying goodbye—the grieved imagination of a distraught mother. Yet there it was again, a breeze that brushed at the sting of drying tears on my cheek.

Is He here? Is God here?

It was time. I realized that even the breeze was another loving nudge from my merciful Father God. How else would the ashes have blown across the pond without landing in a clump at the edge of the bank? God had thought of everything.

CHAPTER 16:

EMPTY POCKET

(2009)

G od not only showed up in 2009, but He revealed Himself masterfully whenever I called on Him. It wasn't until 2009 that I had grown enough in my maturity as a Christian that I finally felt ready to let Nathanael go. In the post-abortive years, I had needed to hold on to something, anything about the pregnancy that everyone else had forgotten. A pregnancy without a child is like a secret that is never told. No one ever asked how many pregnancies I'd had, but rather how many children I'd successfully shepherded to earth. Sadly, the only place where my secret son was ever disclosed was on new patient intake forms at a medical office. There were usually two questions. One asked how many pregnancies I had with a tiny, dashed line into which a single digit barely fit.

___# pregnancies?

___# of live births/# of children?

Sometimes the forms were a bit kinder and broader in their questioning. I imagined some women skipped this part of the medical forms, and others hastily filled in the blanks because the answers were so simple. Every time I completed this section on a form, I wished so much that the two questions would match. Pregnancies – 2. Children – 2. I decided the question was not only cruel but that it wasn't relevant for many medical specialties outside of obstetrics and gynecology. I wasn't making an argument that this question should be banned on all medical forms, but it was a poignant example of how seemingly trivial things in loss or trauma could be a trigger for a post-abortive mother. Each time I ran across this question staring up at me in black and white, it was as if the form was asking me, *So, what's it gonna be? Are you gonna be honest on this form or are you planning to lie this time?*

Perhaps the easiest thing to do was to skip this section on the forms. After all, I could conscientiously object to hundreds of other written and behavioral requests in the workplace and the world. I tried this experiment twice. One time I hastily skipped the question, dabbed my eyes, and returned the form to the receptionist with my usual lipstick-laden smile. When the medical assistant later roomed me before the doctor came in, she didn't even look at my forms, nor did the doctor that day. I gathered my purse and jacket to leave the exam room after the appointment, and I rode the elevator down to the parking garage, leaning against the cold metal handrail thinking, *they didn't ask me about the spot I left blank on the form.* My son felt relegated to a blank spot, an empty spot, an empty pocket in my heart.

Empty pocket in my heart

You are a pocket in my heart
that will never
be stitched shut.

You are an ache in my gut
every time I remember
the plans I made for you.

You are the movement
of the leaves and grasses
when the wind blows.

The gentle push and pull between the big wind
accompanied by the silent after breeze
that rustles only the most tender grass.

ᴄᴔ Journal entry (June 2000)

For me, the question, "How many pregnancies have you had?" seemed
to come out of nowhere like an unexpected flashlight shining on a closely
held secret. The question dared to ask something that for some women was
unspeakable. When I encountered this insensitive question on a medical
form my response typically paralleled where I was in the grief process. In
the early years after my abortion, the question quickly filled my eyes with
tears as if someone had squeezed a lemon in front of my face. As late
as 2009, during an office visit with a new endocrinologist, I played with
euphemisms, trying to find a nice way to answer truthfully. Despite the leap
of healing that followed scattering Nathanael's ashes, shortly thereafter I
ushered in the angry phase of grief. At medical appointments, I wanted to
scratch out the whole pregnancy section on the form with the cheap pens
they provided. I'd been asked this question in person and face-to-face many
times, most often by a medical assistant who was busy typing my vitals into
an exam room computer.

"How many pregnancies then?" usually a female MA would ask.

I wanted to have a quick, tidy answer bereft of any emotion, like "Two
pregnancies. One daughter."

By being brief and to the point, I'd hoped it sent the message that I was
a closed book to any follow-up questions. I found it easier to answer within
a gynecological setting where compassion ran high. In a female-dominated
space, I could more comfortably lengthen my answer to, "Two pregnancies.
One daughter. Second trimester loss." Thankfully only one male physician
was nosy enough to ask—Dr. Rouesch, an orthopedist.

"It says here you had two D&E procedures in 2000. You mean
one, right?"

I felt my cheeks burn with a rush of anger as I imagined answering with a tone as frigid as my feelings. But, predictably polite in public, I answered demurely.

"No. I had medical complications with my second pregnancy."

I sat there puzzled as to why, in an era when some people were offended by the improper use of a particular pronoun, no one seemed offended by a question that was directly asking, "Did all your pregnancies result in living children?" No one conspired to be cruel during the medical intake process. None of them meant to hurt my feelings, until I met Dr. Rouesch. I was seeing him related to sacroiliac (SI) joint hypermobility and dysfunction on referral from my primary care doctor. The pain was persistent, had interrupted my love of running, and was spreading to include a burning feeling that went down my buttocks and to the outside of my hip and thigh. Unfortunately, it was significantly impacting my daily life. Dr. Rouesch ordered a basic hip x-ray and came into the room as if he was inconvenienced by my appointment.

Before introducing himself, he said, "Your hip x-ray looks fine. Nothing to do here."

I responded politely and told him that I wanted to get back to running and be able to sit in my chair at work longer than thirty minutes at a time. He flipped through my intake forms, looking pained, sighing as he crossed his legs awkwardly in green medical scrubs.

"So, the pregnancy loss was in 2000?" He looked up from his bifocals.

I nodded sheepishly.

"You know that kind of procedure coupled with the ligament laxity that comes with pregnancy can cause a lot of women to have this kind of nebulous sacroiliac pain. If the pain has gone on this long, perhaps you should consider a psychiatric evaluation to be sure you're over the grief process." He closed my file and looked directly at me from under his surgical cap that he hadn't bothered to remove.

I took his comments as my cue to gather my things, and I bid him goodbye with my default autopilot, regularly described in my medical records as "Mrs. Harper is a very pleasant young woman." My parting words to him were limited to thanking him, in spite of his comments making me feel like a complete disaster. I wasn't a fan of wasting medical resources, but I got a referral to a psychiatrist solely for the purpose of a full psychiatric evaluation. It was a comprehensive and honest report, describing me as a "little tense" but "high functioning" without any diagnosis codes listed other than the one I had told him about, namely PTSD. During the interview and evaluation by the psychiatrist he asked me several questions about any pregnancy losses, but I must have passed the test because nothing was written about it in his narrative summary. I knew it was a passive-aggressive move, but I took a copy of the psych eval and hand delivered it to Dr. Rouesch's office several weeks later with a cover letter inside that read,

> *"For your reading pleasure. Apparently, my SI joint pain is unrelated to my pregnancy loss, as indicated in the attached psych eval. Your comments during my office visit when you didn't know anything about my situation were deeply hurtful. I'm glad you don't spend much time at patient bedsides, because I left your office without help or any shred of human kindness."*

There was no doubt that I was deep into the weeds of the anger stage of the grief process at that time. Scattering the ashes at the pond had loosened the stranglehold of shame that I felt around my neck, and while the release I felt in letting go of the ashes was real, I was only just learning that trauma was an onion of many layers, where a mix of feelings can twist together and stack one on top of another. Anger on top of shame, defense mechanisms on top of coping strategies, each one holding the other in place, not unlike the stack of sweatshirts that had fallen on my head that telling day in my closet.

CHAPTER 17:

GRIEF

(2017)

The leading researchers on the grief process cite how the initial phases of denial and shock serve a logical purpose to protect and energize the bereaved enough to engage in survival mode. The early experience of grief can afford people the ability to take care of business and survive the initial days of trauma on pure adrenalin.

Regardless of where someone is in the grief, recovery, and healing process after trauma, I believe there are two primary states of being in which the bereaved can exist. Simply put, I call one functional and the other dysfunctional. I have a friend who tragically lost her young daughter in a sudden and unexpected way that seems incomprehensible. It was nothing she or her family could prepare for, and people who know anything about her story of loss feel her child's death was not only tragic but unjust. She inspires me daily with her strength and her ability to live in a functional state. As much as losing an unborn child in a traumatic way changed me, I cannot fathom how deep and gaping the hole in one's soul must be after suffering the loss of a child who was born alive and was known. Losing a child is not the natural order of things, and parents struggle to go on when their child's life has ended too soon.[2]

On rare occasions, I will have a vivid flash in my mind that something bad has happened to my girls, although they are adults living away from home. These flashes feel like punches to the gut, a bit like free-falling down a steep roller coaster track. I feel a visceral tightness under my sternum in the top of my stomach often followed by a few tears. My breathing becomes tight, and I have to stop the thought, take a breath, and assure myself that my girls are fine. These miniature panic attacks, sponsored by motherhood, immediately compel me to say a prayer, and most of the time some peace washes over me, and I can return to reality. It is incomprehensible to imagine what life would be like without my daughters. Would the grief of losing them grip me like a strangling anxiety attack without end? I'm thankful that God has spared me the experience of trying to live in the wake of losing my grown children with whom I have created a deep bond of intense love and cherished memories. I am sure that I could not bear it, and that I would linger indefinitely in a state of dysfunctional grief. I have seen a few people in my life who live in a reality after loss that is so dark and disabling that hopelessness, depression, and brokenness define their days. A person unable to initiate coping strategies and accept help and resources can get stuck in a dysfunctional grief pattern, and for them I am moved to deep compassion.

I look at the functional reality of grief as survivorship, made possible by a variety of coping skills, one of which is the gift of compartmentalization. The functional survivor appears to be high-functioning on the outside—well-groomed and participating in self-care, often working in a career, vocation, ministry, or as a volunteer. They participate in life, complete the tasks that are given to them or initiated on their own, have friends, create new memories, eat, sleep, breathe, and live. When operating in this outwardly functional reality, it's possible that no one would know they are living with grief. They know how to take steps forward each day, living their life and caring for their spouse, their children, and friends. Their loss neither defines nor controls them.

In both realities of a functional and dysfunctional grief life, there exist percentages of function and dysfunction. I imagine that my reaction to losing a child would be to fall into a dysfunctional reality and never find my way out, but this dismal scenario rarely includes God. Even for someone who remains deep in a pit of despair and is not outwardly functional, there can be glimmers of hope, thoughts of future plans, time spent enjoying an event, a television program, a book, or a meal that entices them to peek out of their cocoon to see the light going on around them. The same is true of the functional person for whom life is streaming along. They can sink into invisible darkness and take a turn back on the bicycle of grief at any time. The functionally bereaved travel through valleys, as all people do. There are so many books written on grief and loss because it is a complex topic in the emotional, physical, psychological, and spiritual realms. What else within the human experience can so profoundly change a person as the loss of a loved one?

Death means separation from someone with whom we were in relationship. The Bible defines death as separation from God. "But your iniquities have separated you from God; your sins have hidden his face from you, so that he will not hear." (Isaiah 59:2) Even Jesus who was fully man and fully God wept at the death of His friend, Lazarus, seen in (John 11:35). Jesus cried out in the Garden of Gethsemane with such intensity before His crucifixion that He sweated drops of blood in (Luke 22:44). In the end, Jesus cried out in pain and anguish on the cross before His separation from Father God—separation from His beloved. Jesus knew the outcome of the gospel, and yet He experienced pain and grief when facing the ultimate brutal death of crucifixion.

When we let go of a baby who has yet to be born, we grieve expectations, hopes, and dreams. Unlike grief for someone with whom we have walked this planet for a time, grief for an unborn child who has died means mourning someone our body and heart loved but our eyes did not yet see.

One year I started working through a Bible study on the topic of abortion healing called, *Surrendering the Secret* by Pat Layton. The author posed the question, "What might happen if we choose to intentionally remember the past and understand more about that day, that choice, when life changed forever?" I sat with this prickly question for a few minutes, and I thought back to how intentional I had been about scheduling my grief for "appropriate" times after my daughter was asleep, or on the annual anniversary of my son's would-be birthday. I was perplexed by the author of the study asking me to go back in time to the abortion experience. What value was there in revisiting the strong emotions of anxiety, grief, regret, sadness, and shame? Feeling rebellious, I pressed on to the next page of the study guide, hoping the author would answer my question. Pat went on to ask how I thought the approach of being intentional about remembering could be more effective in my healing. She compared superficial healing to true healing. I had to admit I was stumped. I put my head down on my study guide and the only thing that came to mind was the overused metaphor of the layers of an onion. Intellectually I understood that only superficial healing was possible if I peeled back just the outer skin and the first layer of the onion. There were so many more layers to explore.

I was proud of how I'd given myself an "A" in grief. I'd participated in an online community with other parents who had made the same agonizing choice, and I bought a locket to wear when I wanted to feel close to my lost infant. I set up a box in which to put the tiny urn of his ashes, along with the ultrasound picture, a pair of his never-worn newborn shoes, fall leaves from my annual visits to his pond in November, and a few poems I'd written about him. *How many people did all that?* Surely, I had been a grief overachiever.

The many books on grief and counselors I consulted suggested memorializing an unborn baby as part of the healing process. Culturally we do this with people who are born alive and who were known before death, but it was freeing to read books and blogs that recommended this practice for the unborn as well. After the memorial paver was removed from the park there were several years where I felt adrift on Nathanael's anniversary. I still needed a tangible memorial for my son.

Through my ongoing reading I learned about the National Memorial for the Unborn in Chattanooga, Tennessee. It is a memorial founded in 1994 to create a place dedicated to providing families and those affected by miscarriage and abortion with a physical location to visit to honor their unborn children. The grounds house a Wall of Names where anyone who has lost a baby to abortion may come to honor their child in the hope of deeper comfort and healing. I decided to purchase a brass plaque for installation on the Wall of Names as a fitting and permanent memorial to the baby boy I was never to meet but who forever changed my life. It reads

Nathanael M. Harper
11:11 2000
Angel in Heaven

Nathanael of the Bible only made a brief appearance in all of scripture in John chapter 1 and 21, not unlike the short-lived story of my baby, but the assurance of knowing I will see him again was a balm for my grief.

CHAPTER 18:

ONLY SAY THE WORD

(2018)

I leaned back into the wooden pew, frustrated that the bench didn't meet the small of my perpetually sore lower back. To take the edge off the pain, I took the brown wool dress coat off my lap and mangled it into a lumpy ball behind me. Now I could breathe, in and out, though never deeply lest my stomach stick out in public. It was 2018, and I felt at home in my evangelical church community of almost eighteen years. The tiny square of commercialized communion host was pressed hard between the palm and pinky of my left hand. I never felt comfortable fingering it with unclean hands like so many did, and while I had never caught a cold after communion, I only half believed the holy elements afforded supernatural protection. Part of the doubting Thomas in me didn't know if it was spiritual immunity or my germaphobia that kept me well. It was deeply instilled in childhood, during my school days, that my hands were neither worthy nor clean enough to hold the heavenly host.

In my life as a Christian, while each communion experience was special at the time, they had begun to run together after years of enjoying the freedom of partaking in communion. We sang the favorite hymn of our beloved pastor who had passed away from the inhumane disease of ALS (Lou Gehrig's disease). It was a powerful morning of praise and worship, and I listened intently to our new pastor deftly sharing the story of the Last Supper, as he reverently held up the cup of metaphorical wine. I felt the plastic cup of grape juice in the fingers of my right hand, held delicately like an egg, not too tightly lest it crack, and not too loosely or I'd be trying to bleach a purple stain out of my shoes when I got home. I closed my eyes, feeling tremendous awe at the honor being able to receive communion, and it also helped me slow my racing mind. I focused on each word he said, as he read from Matthew 26.

"Let's eat together as we remember the sacrifice Christ made for us all." I bowed my head, gingerly dropping the now-sweaty square of the host into my mouth.

I took a deep breath through my nose and before I'd broken it with my teeth, the responsorial from the Catholic masses of my childhood queued up, as if the priests of my past had pushed play on a cassette tape.

Lord, I am not worthy to receive you, but only say the word and I shall be healed.

I had never meditated before on what I was saying, but as I thought about these words, I stopped short.

Wait, but Lord, You made me worthy, so I am worthy now, right?

I began an internal wrestling match in my mind, causing me to miss the cue to drink the cup of communion juice. I tossed it back like a shot, awkwardly moved it to my left hand, and jumped back into the silent internal debate in my head.

Where did that come from—am I worthy? My brain was racing and jumping from thought to thought.

Should I stop saying this memorized response when I take communion? I mean the second half is right. In a word, in an instant, in Your death, Jesus, You healed me and forgave me of my sins. ALL of my sins—past, present, and future, right? I opened my eyes to make sure I hadn't said that out loud, but many of those around me were still in prayer.

Though I felt the awkward jacket mound behind my back, my mind traveled back to 1983, where I could smell candles and the faint aroma of cloves, orrisroot, and orange from a gold pomander. The varnished pew of my daydream felt cold on the back of my thighs just above my uniform-approved knee socks. Before the monsignor cued us to stand, a lone singer stood up to chant a familiar melancholy melody.

"When we eat this bread and drink this cup, we proclaim Your death, Lord Jesus, until You come in glory...until You come in glory."

The priest directed us to enter into silent prayer. His green robe of brocaded satin moved fluidly and silently. The only sound was of the carefully placed steps of his sensible black shoes. He turned to face us, revealing the Latin peace sign, *Pax Mundi*, embroidered in gold thread. He walked to the altar again without a sound, as if his life depended on the silence that hung in the church. A dutiful altar boy brought him the elements from a shrouded side table. A heavy golden goblet stood conspicuously absent from its home beside the ceremoniously large monstrance of hammered metal. The priest set it down gently and soundlessly upon the unblemished white linen cloth. Our officiant, the monsignor who was a special guest that day, unfolded the holy host wrapped in pressed fabric: the first fold he made away from him and the second fold toward him. He quickly knelt before the host and crossed himself, then he stood upright again, once more denoting the sign of the cross—Father, Son, and Holy Spirit. He wiped the goblet carefully with a clean white linen, ensuring it lay perfectly flat across the cup.

"Lamb of God, You take away the sins of the world, have mercy on us. Lamb of God, You take away the sins of the world, have mercy on us. Lamb of God, You take away the sins of the world, grant us peace."

There was not a sound anywhere in the church, such that the snap of the wafer being broken in two was deafening.

"The Lord be with you," he continued.

"And also with you, the respondents offered back.

"Let us offer each other the sign of peace," and before he could finish, I watched as the amalgam of parishioners from my past exchanged the customary sign of peace. In my daydream, the priest invited the attendees to come forward to receive the Holy Communion. A peace washed over me as I watched the mass in my mind come to a close. While my vision was neither complete nor ceremonially accurate, the feeling of reverence it elicited in my heart was the same now, as I sat in my 2018 church pew, as it was when I was a schoolgirl.

Communion changed early in my Catholic school experience—no longer in Latin, with the added relief that my friends could receive the communion wafer in their hands, rather than having to stick out their tongues. The few times I slipped into the communion line, I took great care to cup my hand beneath my open palm, creating a throne for the holy host, just as I had watched my friends do it—until I was forbidden by Sister Zip Zip.

My husband, Garrett suddenly put his hand on my leg, jolting me back to the present with his cue that he wanted me to pray with him in response to the communion I had already eaten without him, lost in my private world of Catholic school flashbacks. The worship team of our church was comprised of musicians on drums, two keyboards, a trumpet, and a bass guitar, along with three singers—startling in its stark contrast to the nostalgic and quiet mass of my childhood. My adult church experience was significantly different than my parochial education, but the act of communion always brought me to a reverent connection with Jesus. Our church didn't require that we stand up during the singing of praise and worship songs, but I wanted to. We were singing one of my favorite contemporary songs, and others in my church family jumped in with a chorus of clapping and dancing in place. I felt free to sing and free to lift my hands in uninhibited worship to the Lord I loved. Though Jesus and I didn't have a proper introduction until 2000, I had loved God all my life. I could finally pray and sing freely in a large group, I was reading my Bible regularly, and I had been in a Bible study class for ten years. I knew God loved me, and, academically, I knew that Christ died for all, and that included me.

Lord, I am not worthy to receive You, but only say the word and I shall be healed. These words from my past ran through my head on a continuous loop, even while I was singing and gently bouncing in the pew.

Why am I not worthy? The thought felt oddly convicting and made my eyes sting.

I knew why. I knew why I considered others worthy yet at times I felt worthless. A pit of tension began to build in my stomach.

Only say the word—the word. The Word with a capital "W" was supposed to be His Holy Book, the Bible. Healing could have referred to how instantaneous it's supposed to be when we are transformed from imperfect, mortal bodies to restored and eternal bodies. I made a note to study this further. Yet I knew that scholarly study of the scriptures wouldn't answer this morning's revelation. "The word" that held me back from worthiness was the word I could not speak.

Abortion. I heard a dark whisper in my mind that ended with a hiss.

I had worked diligently in my growth as a Christian to overcome feelings of shame related to my sins, my divorce, my lack of purity in relationships, so many things. I believed that He died for all people and for all sins. Yet I held tightly to a personal fear that Jesus died for all sins except my abortion. While I held no judgment against other women who had made the abortion choice, I had reserved judgment for myself that was unyielding. The word that stood in the way of my spiritual development was revealed that day through a daydream of a communion responsorial from my past.

Only say the word. It became personalized in that moment, as I talked to myself.

Only say the word. Sitting there, I knew that if I confessed the word "abortion" to God with a repentant heart, He would forgive me.

The person who needed to break the years of silence was me. If only I could say the word out loud to myself, to God, to one person. After my abortion, I lashed myself to the camp of the unworthy, where I was sure

I belonged forever. I encased myself in the secrecy of a tomb of my own making. Silence kept the secrets. Secrets reinforced the shame. Shame put me into emotional isolation. I knew I had to pick up a chisel and begin to break my way out. The first step was the hardest. Before Jesus could speak His Word over me so that I could be healed, I had to say "the word" myself.

I excused myself from the pew before the closing prayer and went out to sit in our parked car. I stared out the window, waiting for Garrett to finish visiting with church friends. The heavy rain appeared white against the dark green of the cedar trees.

"I had an abortion." I whispered out loud, my breath fogging up the glass of the car window. As the words left my mouth, they rose up from the inside of my throat like the blades of an electric mixer.

I said it again and again and again, each time with a slightly stronger voice until tears began to flow, and for once I didn't care if anyone heard me in my silent tomb or in the car of our church parking lot. I just knew I wanted out—finally.

The following morning, I had a scheduled appointment with a new counselor who worked close to my office. A previous counselor I had seen for a few months right after the abortion focused on what she felt was PTSD from abortion trauma and medical malpractice. This new woman was plain in her appearance but kind, and like most practitioners, she asked how many children I had in the early establishment of our relationship. *How was I supposed to answer her?* Social norms told me to stick to one of three multiple-choice answers based directly on the level of intimacy I shared with the person who was asking.

Until this particular Monday, sitting in a counseling office so small that it felt like a dimly lit closet, I hadn't told anyone but immediate family the full and ragged truth. This new counselor was older, with short, frosted hair and ice-blue eyes, and she looked at me attentively and with a soft countenance. I realized that day that I was still angry. I didn't want to hurt her intentionally, but my tongue was like a sharp sword, and I wanted to cut someone with my words. I wanted to shock someone into having to hear and stomach the truth of my word choices. I knew there was a word I had come to say.

I'd spent years trying to stuff the decision I made that day, and I finally wanted to invite someone else into the burden. I felt less guilty with my honesty because at least she was being paid to listen to me. On some level I thought that if I shared the most unedited version of the truth, it might take some of the toxin out of the trauma.

So, I took a shallow breath, looking up from my lap into her eyes, and I said, "I killed my baby. I had an abortion."

She didn't even flinch.

I continued. "It's called medical termination to make it sound easier than it is. It's supposed to make me feel better about my choice. No one gave us another choice."

I stopped, waiting for her to gasp or something, but she didn't. I had never used the word abortion publicly before, because somehow the fact that I was married and was a loving mother who wanted this baby, meant that I did not fit the abortion stereotype. In my mind women who had abortions were usually young, sometimes hindered in their ability to pursue advanced education, and often had no support system. I assumed many women who chose abortion were unable to provide financially for a child, or perhaps felt forced to choose between ending a pregnancy or ending a career. I had seen a documentary in college about a segment of woman who had serial abortions as a form of birth control, and I didn't identify with those women at all. Perhaps some women felt forced into abortion by an unsupportive partner or controlling parents. TV typically chose to portray women having abortions walking up to abortion clinics in scenes complete with pro-life petitioners holding up signs, and that surely wasn't me. I had a surgical "procedure" in a metropolitan hospital.

These pictures in my head didn't fit. We weren't too young. We were well educated. I had a significant support system. I was married, and we could provide financially for our baby. My career was on hold at the time so I could stay home with our toddler, and I had abandoned plans to go to graduate school. I had never chosen abortion as a birth control option, and my husband wanted this baby as much as I did. What was my excuse? Was it right to say that the list of reasons a woman might have an abortion were excuses? If an excuse can give rise to a pardon, surviving an abortion was anything but a pardon. It felt like a life sentence of soul damage.

I told this new counselor that I wanted to be honest with her. I told her I was tired of lying to everyone who asked me the question about how I lost my baby.

I told her, "I didn't lose the baby like a wallet."

I told her that at sixteen-and-a-half weeks our baby boy was found to have severe congenital malformations, and multiple medical providers, including my OB-GYN and a geneticist, promptly and definitively recommended that we terminate the pregnancy. They used words like "medical termination," and because it all happened in a blurry haze, my mind treated it like it was just another medical diagnosis from which I was expected to emerge a survivor.

I was usually quick to build rapport with anyone, but I knew I was holding back certain parts of my story with this counselor. She used an emerging technique at the time called EMDR, Eye Movement Desensitization and Reprocessing.[3] I told her that the first counselor I'd seen after the loss had also mentioned EMDR and used a tapping technique on my knees. The new counselor was happy I had some familiarity with the research on this form of therapy, which might have sounded strange to those who hadn't heard of it. Rather than tapping, she used a bar of lights on which the bulbs lit up one by one from left to right. I was to learn to follow the movements of the lights without moving my head. She also wanted me to consider hypnosis, but I told her that because I was intensely hypervigilant, I wouldn't be able to relax or be open to suggestions in such an environment.

"Do you feel ready to give EMDR a try today? she asked at my second appointment. I hesitated long enough to feel the familiar knot of anxiety forming in my stomach.

"Sure. You seem to have a lot of questions about my childhood. Do we start there?"

"Well, given that you've indicated you can't commit to this process for more than about three months, I think we should start with a very short memory about the loss of your baby, since you said that's what brought you in to see me." She repositioned her weight in the pale blue wingback chair and looked at me intently with her aged face, her skin looking a bit like softened butter.

"Umm, I don't know. I try to only go there in my head once a year in November, the day I honor him, or sometimes if a certain song comes on." I uncrossed my legs and felt awkward with my feet flat on the floor.

"You've been very honest and raw with me about what happened, so I know you're brave. Can you pick a small memory, maybe one that's just before the abortion? For example, the car ride to the hospital or maybe the admitting process when you arrived?"

"I wrote all this out right after it happened. Isn't that enough?" I crossed my legs again, well aware that I was trying to close my body up tightly to avoid her prying questions.

"Why don't we start the EMDR lights and take about five minutes to relax into the couch, and when you're ready, just say okay. Then begin to focus on the lights and breathe. I will ask questions to learn more about what you are seeing. You can stop at any time."

I felt like yelling at her, "Of course, I can stop at any time! I'm paying you, and I'm not a prisoner."

Instead, I answered, "Okay. I'll try," in a half-hearted and quiet voice, already distracted by the ping pong ball-sized orange lights that began to travel back and forth along the light bar with a mesmerizing rhythm.

The sound of a bird outside landing on the rain gutter startled me. I refocused again on the frustrating ball of light traveling back and forth to the right, left, right.

"Okay. I'm done." I broke my gaze away from the light bar and reached to the floor for the familiarity of my purse. "Sorry, I can't focus that long."

"You did really well. You seemed deeply focused on following the light for about two minutes without breaking gaze."

Let's call the local newspaper, I thought to myself, internally mocking her ridiculous praise.

"Can you tell me if a memory came to mind? Can you describe it?"

"It was kind of like a flashback I get sometimes. I don't know what triggers it."

"How often would you say you have flashbacks about the abortion?" I couldn't answer her question quickly because I was distracted and annoyed by her flippant use of the word *abortion*.

Who was she to keep calling it that?

"Umm...not often. Maybe a few times a year in a dream when I'm waking up, and once in the middle of a long meeting at work. Oh, and every time I listen to his song. And I guess every time I see the pro-life demonstrators on the highway holding up those awful signs with pictures of dead fetuses on them. And I guess I should tell you, most of the time when I have a surgery or a medical procedure." I'd shared too much, and I began digging in my purse again, this time for my tinted lip balm.

Perhaps it was three months of EMDR or the approach of my 40 birthday, but I began to admit on rare occasion that I had a secret child. In an intimate setting, like a women's retreat when someone spoke about a miscarriage, I was sometimes willing to say, "Me too." Perhaps it was my regret that Lily had been sealed into the fate of being an only child, and I felt profoundly guilty that her family was broken by divorce. I desperately wanted to have more children, and everyone I knew seemed to have kids popping out of the doors and windows of their minivans. Frenzied mom friends were perpetually running kids from swim practice and cheer camp to soccer games. It was natural when a new mom I'd meet would ask how many kids I had, and I'd say, "one." Most mother peers replied politely to my short answer, permitting me to stay in the unspoken mom club, but my heart felt a little *less than*.

One of the ministries where I volunteered brought young mothers together with older moms to a weekly brunch of socializing and meaningful guest speakers. At the start of the year, we gave the moms a slew of ribbons and special pens, scrapbooking stickers, and artful paper goods with which to complete a simple craft project of making their own name tags. We encouraged them to put a pink or blue bead on their name tags to identify how many kids they had, and we did the same in making our name tags as leaders. It was a sweet, meaningful, and simple exercise—simple, until the first time I had to explain what the pink and blue beads were for, when I was also supposed to tell them that the white beads were for any children they had in heaven. There was an unspoken respect between the mothers that meant we fully acknowledged all of our children, not just the ones who were living.

My first year, as I was helping a new mom make her nametag, the young woman observantly motioned to my nametag, acknowledged my white bead and said, "I'm sorry that you lost a baby." For women like me and others, the word used to acknowledge missing babies is "lost." No one means anything cruel by it, but that day her observation was followed with a nervous second question. "When was your miscarriage?"

The assumption of miscarriage is powerful. In our world and especially in our church communities, miscarriage is often assumed to be the only means of infant loss. While stillbirth is less common than miscarriage, my heart aches for these mothers who are rarely acknowledged.[4] Miscarriage is often unspoken or softly whispered, though it accounts for 10-25% of pregnancies in the United States.[5] The Centers for Disease Control (CDC) reports as recently as 2018 that apparently 42% of unintended pregnancies in the U.S. are aborted,[6] and The Guttmacher Institute validates that approximately 25% of women in the U.S. will undergo an abortion before the age of 45.[7] This is a large segment of our female population, but why are our lips pursed in silence, seemingly devoid of empathy? These statistics represent real people—perhaps our own mothers, sisters, daughters, nieces, and friends. Abortion is rarely mentioned publicly outside of polarized and inflammatory news reports, and the silence is deafening within many church communities. Once we hear the word abortion, listening stops, dialogue dies, and isolation sets in. With silence comes shame, and shame can lead abortion survivors to question their worth. If they question their worth, they may question their right to enter into church membership, and from the outside looking in, it can be hard to imagine being forgiven by a Savior who died for all people and for all sins. As one of these women who migrated from outside to inside the church and lived in silence about my past, I found that wearing a white bead on my nametag afforded me the dignity that my deceased baby was real.

CHAPTER 19:

POCKET FULL OF POSIES

(2018)

Had I fallen asleep? I startled and felt a deep chill inside my coat. The bench must have been damp, and my jeans felt wet and uncomfortable. I had been praying, or so I thought. I felt sick and alone, and I no longer wanted to linger amidst the beauty of this familiar park. It was time to go home and admit that this year at the pond was neither tender nor healing. It just was. The gazebo was only a short walk ahead of me, and I had been at this barren place in my heart many times before. There was a dark enemy who worked hard to keep me tangled in the weeds of grief, and I had no intention of letting him win again. The view across the pond never disappointed, and this anniversary visit was no different. I closed my eyes and asked God to take me back to the day He met me here in 2009, and to spare me from ever going back to the trauma of post-surgical recovery rooms. I wanted to remember the day that this pond had brought me closer to the peace of letting go.

↬ Journal entry (November 2016)

Nathanael, "Natty," would have been eighteen this year. As I made my annual pilgrimage to the park on that sunny but blustery November afternoon, I didn't feel like listening to the song that had become "his" song.

It was the first time I hadn't felt a strong pull to get to the park in a hurry. My emotions felt rather flat, but I knew I needed to make some quiet time for prayer and reflection. I had given up any expectations of hearing from God on this matter or feeling the comforting soft fingers of the wind on my cheek that my imagination clung to as the spirit presence of my son. I felt the weak warmth of the sun streaming through the sunroof merge with the heat blowing on my cold feet. The leaves fell fast from the trees as I drove, and it looked like they were running furiously across the highway to avoid me hitting them.

Several counselors with whom I'd developed varying degrees of relationships over the last decade, ran through my mind, and I heard one of their voices ask me, *How are you feeling?* I pretended that I owed the voice in my head some kind of answer, and I rolled my eyes, knowing this would probably be a prudent way to start my annual journey to the pond. I mentally searched through the file cabinets in my mind for something, a memory, a feeling, an answer, but only one thing came. As I made the familiar turn at the stoplight to exit the highway and get onto the country lane to the park, my answer to the imaginary counselor was a question, not an answer.

Why am I not over this yet? It's been eighteen years! I exhaled in a giant sigh, feeling exasperated, and making my turn with more speed than I needed.

I parked my Jeep and gathered my phone, headphones, and grey knit cap and separated the key fob from my giant mound of keys. I'd learned after all these years to travel light for the walk to the pond. One year I tried to go without my cell phone to practice mindfulness, but the park was too beautiful in November to skip taking a few photos. I tried listening to his song on my earbuds as I walked up the pathway to the pond's edge. Nothing. No feelings. No tears. Not even a catch of sentiment in my throat. I walked neither fast nor slow, but with a learned intent, and unlike in years past, the other park visitors were invisible to me. Thankfully, there weren't any ne'er-do-wells in the gazebo, my gazebo, as if it were reserved for me every year on this date like season tickets. I felt rather salty, and I wasn't sure that my polite default would have been patient about waiting for my turn to sit on the gazebo bench for my annual scan of the pond. The gazebo was empty, and I sat, and I sat, getting colder and colder as the wind was rudely telling the sun who was in charge of the temperature this late in the year. I closed my eyes and waited for a prayer to come, and because I was so cold, I started it silently in my mind on autopilot. Getting started was always the hardest part, just like exercise, but my prayer quickly morphed into a prayer directed to my son, something that had never happened before. Startled, I quickly recanted.

Sorry, God. That was weird of me to start talking to Natty in the middle of our talk.

It seemed that God was okay with my free associations, because I felt a layer of warmth come over me in spite of how cold I was, and I continued on with the monologue to Natty in my mind. I asked him if he was okay. A catch in my throat arrived right on cue. I felt tears coming as I told him I still missed him as much eighteen years later as I did on the day I said goodbye to him. I quickly opened my eyes to reorient myself to avoid crying. The ducks I'd grown accustomed to seeing at the pond swam in little clusters, creating circles of ripples around their bobbing bodies. I realized I had something in common with them, the way I was calm and composed on the outside but furiously paddling on the invisible underside. Maybe I would get a sign from God this year like a butterfly or a bird landing on the park bench beside me.

Anything, please, Lord?

Nine years before, when I had scattered Natty's ashes at the pond, it was an afternoon just like this one, an apple cider autumn kind of day. The grass, always green year-round, created a sharp contrast against the rich autumn colors of deep red, orange, and what seemed dozens of vibrant shades of yellow. Living in evergreen terrain, I was still surprised every fall by the hidden trees that conspicuously showed themselves. The cold wind came again and crept intrusively into the gaps between my coat buttons and the lines within my tightly wrapped scarf, making my bones ache at much too early an age. Yet the sun cast its brilliance upon the pond—his pond—turning the wake from the string of playful ducks into a heavenly illusion of diamond water skippers. Surprisingly, every year on the eleventh of November, the notorious Northwest weather cooperated. I took it as a gentle hug from God that He was present, no matter how alone I felt on this melancholy anniversary.

A beloved high school teacher's reminder of the concept of mindfulness came to mind, but for me the act of mindfulness could only be achieved by a kind of mindlessness. Perpetually hard on myself, I was my own worst enemy. Individual prayer with God did not often come easily. I thought about how embarrassed I was last week when praying out loud in my car as I said, "Thank You, Lord, for this day and for our many blessings [PERIOD]. In Your Son's name [COMMA], Amen." I had literally dictated this prayer using Siri voice recognition out of habit from one too many daily voice texts on my cell phone while driving. I was sure that God had a sense of humor, but the enemy immediately deflected my apology and accused me of being bad at prayer.

"I can't even pray right," I chastised myself.

When I was able to focus, prayer was the only comforting experience connected to the trauma and regret. I was thankful for God's presence, a presence I no longer questioned or doubted that I deserved.

My big toes had grown numb, and the familiar sound of a runner's feet striking the asphalt behind the gazebo interrupted my third prayer attempt. I looked up at the jogger and felt the familiar tug of jealousy about the day I had to hang up my own running shoes from painful joint hypermobility. The jogger reminded me that my daughter needed new running shoes, and that if I made it back to town before five o'clock, I could pay for the ones on hold at our local sporting goods store.

Stop! Exasperated by how difficult I found it to focus on only one thing, I decided that perhaps this year's Remembrance Day might not be anything to remember.

Hadn't I done the work? I prided myself on being well educated on grief. I had read all the books, joined an online community of mothers enduring neonatal loss, journaled, sought counseling, even faced a lingering diagnosis of PTSD. I took Veterans Day off from my demanding job every year to come to the park to honor my son, my feelings, and the God who saved me.

Then why the flashbacks? I was agitated now.

Anger began to rise up in the back of my throat like bile, and I looked around, thankful that the park seemed empty again.

I am not leaving here without meaning this year! It was a dramatic thought, but it was sincerely me, always questing for closure.

God, why does it feel like even though we dealt with this years ago, You still haven't forgiven me? I fought to hold the tears behind my lashes.

Your Word says that when I repented You scattered my sins as far as the East is from the West. Why won't You let up? Eyelashes betraying me, I felt I was moving into uncharted territory.

"Why can't I forgive myself?" I whispered into my scarf, which had become an oversized tissue.

This was the real question, wasn't it?

It was never God who was holding a grudge. The Jesus who had comforted me in the hospital bed when the nurses and the sedatives could not, He never condemned me. I didn't know if it was the bitterness of my tears or another flashback that caused me to taste the familiar burn of IV morphine in the back of my throat.

Can You forgive me, God? Can I forgive me?

Can you forgive Mommy? A chill ran through my jacket again when I realized what I had just said.

Was I losing my mind? Did I actually just attempt to talk to my lost child? I had done this before, but I was scared I'd said something out loud. I spun my head around like an owl to ensure I was alone. The few people in my life who knew the whole story agreed that this wasn't something a person just "got over" in a few short years, but perhaps I was stuck in some kind of dysfunctional grief loop. I pulled out my cell phone and typed in a quick calendar entry that said, *Schedule counseling appointment.*

It was time to leave the park. It had stirred up dark things in the closet of my heart that were better left alone, but alone was all I felt. I looked up to the clouds in desperation, hoping for some kind of skywriting from God to let me know that my son was okay.

Was there only a thin veil between me and my baby, as I imagined was between me and Christ? How old would my son be in heaven?

If only God would send that familiar whisper on the wind as if to say I was forgiven and that Natty was at peace.

I put my back to the gazebo and headed to my car feeling empty, but most of all lonely. This year's visit had been a disaster of emotional ups and downs. I was glad to put another year between me and the next anniversary of my sweet baby boy.

Emotionally exhausted, I arrived home that evening to an empty house and put a few of the beautiful leaves from the park into Natty's wooden box. I made an unremarkable dinner, exchanged only a few sentences with my daughter who was home from college for a weekend dance with a high school friend. Garrett, who didn't quite know what to do on this day each year, had dutifully put just the right greeting card on my nightstand. I read it and carried it to the drawer in my closet to file it away with the others. Perhaps it was the emptiness of the day, but I pulled out all the Remembrance Day cards from my thoughtful husband and sat on the floor running my fingers over the embossed leaves and tiny adornments until I found the card I wanted. This one was from 2009, the day I had scattered Natty's ashes at the pond. Something about the card reminded me of a poem I had written in my journal right after the abortion. I stared at the orange peel texture on the wall, wishing for an empty house, wishing this day was done.

Still Yet to Come

Would you have known the changing hues of the sky?
as a summer storm moves in.
Or the blurred beauty
of a hummingbird's wings
as it lights upon the flower?

Would your broken heart
have let you feel
the true depth of our love for you?

Would you have fully felt our caresses
across your baby cheeks?
And could you have heard my heartbeat for you
as you slept upon my chest?

We loved you so much
that we could never rob you of
these most precious gifts,
which you deserved to experience and live
the life you were meant to live.

The world that waited for you
abounded with love and wonder.

Our greatest peace comes from knowing
that you knew only love and warmth,
comfort, and no pain and that we protected
you the way that loving parents could.

You have a sister
who is so beautiful and amazing.
It is too great a tragedy to think
you might not have known her fully.

We will always hold you in our hearts
and imagine what it would have been like to
know you.

No matter how tiny and young was your spirit,
you were longed for every day,
and we thank you for the gifts
you have already given us, and the many still yet to come.

✍ Journal entry (June 2000)

CHAPTER 20:

FOR SUCH A TIME AS THIS

(2018)

Later that night the clock illuminated the time, 11:11 p.m., blurry this year since I needed my first pair of mid-life glasses. I'd been plagued by a strange nightly haunting of looking at the nearest clock at precisely 11:11 p.m., and I'd kept this to myself for years. It had become something I tried to avoid, pressing on in my evening work as long as I could before checking the clock as bedtime approached. No matter how busy or distracted I was, if I picked up my cell phone to answer a text, at least once a day the display would announce the time of 11:11. As I faced the clock again that night, I realized this seemingly random habit had begun about nine years ago when Garrett and I were still newly married, living in our first home together as a blended family. The purchase of a different alarm clock for my bedside table when we moved to a new house had not been enough to purge the curious phenomenon, which I explained away as nothing more than a deeply engrained circadian rhythm.

Was it really nine years ago when this 11:11 thing started? I asked myself.

No matter the furious pace of our lives, 11:11 continued to show itself through the clock at work, the clock on the microwave, the watch on my wrist, the time display on my cell phone, the clock in my car, day after day. That night, while brushing my teeth, I looked up from the sink to see the old manual bathroom clock that sat next to the Dixie cups, and there was 11:11 on full display three inches from my face. I stomped downstairs with a spontaneous plan in mind that I thought might fully explain the 11:11 curiosity. I pulled down a family Bible from Garrett's office bookshelf, and I took a seat in his oversized office chair, tearing up bits of Post-It Notes for roughly made bookmarks. I began at (Genesis 11:11) and started reading chapter 11 and verse 11 of every book of the Bible. In the midst of marking each page with a ragged scrap of sticky note, my husband popped his head in to find me reading an old King James Version of a Bible that was not my typical study Bible.

"Are you coming up to bed soon?" he asked innocently, standing in the office doorway in a white t-shirt and shorts with sleepy eyes.

"No. I need to do something. I need some time." I was too engrossed to look up again to say goodnight.

One by one, the eleventh verse of the eleventh chapter of all the books of the Bible came up empty. I made it to (Daniel 11:11 [KJV]), which read, "And the king of the south shall be moved with choler, and shall come forth and fight with him, even with the king of the north: and he shall set forth a great multitude; but the multitude shall be given into his hand." Nope. That didn't seem to have any wisdom or direction for me. I pressed on, though it was almost midnight. (Luke 11:11 [KJV]), "If a son shall ask bread of any of you that is a father, will he give him a stone? or if he ask a fish, will he for a fish give him a serpent?" I wasn't sure what to do with that verse either. I was confident that the powerful and relevant book of Romans would have something for me, but nothing seemed to be applicable in the eleventh chapter of that book either.

Please, God, speak to me through Your Word. Speak to me the way You did to so many people in the Bible. Please, Father God, hear my prayer. I know You must think I'm crazy right now. Believe me, I'm wondering if I've lost my grip. Maybe it seems silly but forgive me for not first thinking I should look in the Bible. I'm sorry I didn't think of this sooner.

I knew that God understood my heart that night. It may have seemed crazy, but I was looking for any word from scripture that could offer comfort, answers, direction, or freedom. My heart sank each time I got to a book that was too short to have eleven chapters. I flipped quickly through Galatians, Ephesians, Philippians, Colossians, 1 Thessalonians, 2 Thessalonians, 1 Timothy, 2 Timothy, Titus, and Philemon. (Hebrews 11:11) spoke of Sarah who was past childbearing age but was later able to bear children because she considered God faithful. At (Revelation 11:11), when I reached the end of my frantic journey for answers, it too failed to offer offered supernatural clarity. I gave up, exhausted.

I shuffled to the bathroom in oversized socks to take my nightly elixir of pills meant to force me into sleep. I longed for the comfort of familiar blankets and the rhythmic sound of my husband's snoring, and I was ready for it to be 11:12 (11/12) in more ways than one. Soon sleep would usher in a new day, and I would head back to the routine of work and the pressure of deadlines. *His mercies are new every morning*, I thought, and I looked forward to things making more sense in the light of day.

My half-asleep husband dutifully asked how it had been at the pond, and he alluded to feeling a bit left out that I always visited the park alone. I was surprised by that, and since he seemed genuinely interested in my response, I decided to be vulnerable and tell him more about the 11:11 hypothesis.

"It was fine. Just kind of an emotionally flat trip this year. You know I go out of respect for God and for Natty, but I usually take away a new insight or a piece of learning, you know?"

"Yeah," he agreed, though I knew he couldn't entirely get it, and that was okay.

"So, there's this thing I haven't told anyone, not even you, because it's weird, honestly so weird," I began at a rapid-fire pace as if to let him know that this was important.

"Okay. What?" he asked, sitting up straight against the pillow to remain alert.

"So…every single night—well, almost every night—whether I'm home or out of town or in my car, studying, picking up my cell phone, walking into any room with a clock, it's 11:11." I looked at him to see if he yet found this fascinating.

"No, you don't get it. I'm not saying that the only time I look at the clock it's 11:11, but let's just say that almost every time no matter where I am, I never miss seeing 11:11 on the clock, and I'm always busy, so I'm not trying to catch this at all."

"That happens to me sometimes, like *déjà vu*," he tried to empathize.

"No! It's NOT *déjà vu*. It's not a feeling that I've been somewhere before. It's like the clock is mocking me to ensure I don't miss 11:11 no matter what I'm doing."

Garrett knew I'd been a science major and that I typically looked for physical and logical explanations for behaviors and patterns in the natural world. He didn't know that no matter how much I actively tried to avoid it, the clock kept betraying me, and my theory of it being a strange coincidence, tied to circadian rhythms or to a subconscious daily habit, didn't explain it away.

"It's honestly creeping me out at this point, and sometimes it feels scary to wake up in the dark, and there it is…11:11 p.m. It started happening during the day, too, though not all the time."

"That is pretty crazy. No, I haven't had that happen I guess."

"The other night I woke up feeling freaked out by it again, and I looked it up on the internet to see if anyone else has this, and there was some pretty weird stuff out there about hauntings and seriously creepy things, and I stopped reading and willed myself to not check the clock at all when I think it's even close to 11:00."

We talked about it for a few more minutes, which led to other sidebars about the dimensions of time, which fascinated Garrett, but he fell asleep, leaving me with my thoughts.

As I settled into the memory foam mattress, something peaceful was descending on me as I reflected on the meaning of Nathanael's birthday as "Remembrance Day," and I began to accept that natural laws and science might not be able to explain my uncanny ability to see a clock wherever I was at 11:11. I was tired enough to take a deep breath and accept that this might have been from God or the universe, or was likely just a habit formed from my own scarred mind.

Leaving for work on November 12, I thought about how odd it seemed that I was just making a connection that these strange nightly 11:11 appearances began in 2009, the year I scattered the baby's ashes at the pond. I was a few minutes late out the door, which meant patiently waiting behind the yellow school bus as it inched its way along the rural route to my office. At the third stop, I couldn't help but enjoy watching the antics of the school kids at the back of the bus fidgeting and tugging at each other's backpacks, and one ornery little pigtailed student stuck her tongue out at me.

Nice, I thought, as the little girl, seemingly raised by wolves, did it again.

I looked around cautiously and stuck my tongue out right back at her. *Why not?* I noticed a brunette boy who was laughing so hard at her antics that his eyes crinkled into tight little almonds.

I wished he looked like Natty, I thought, but he didn't. The bus belched out an enormous cloud of black smoke, and reaching to quickly turn off my heater vents, I nearly had to slam on my brakes.

Why have I never made the connection? Perhaps yesterday's prayers had not gone unheard when I had asked my son at the park if he was okay.

"He's been trying to answer me all these years," I announced out loud in my Jeep.

I didn't go to the park on the eleventh of November because it was Veterans Day or Remembrance Day. I went every year because it was his due date, his anticipated birthday.

"He's been right on time every night at 11:11." I continued my epiphany out loud, relief spreading over me like a soft blanket.

I stopped talking out loud in my car—embarrassed, as if I had been seen by invisible passengers—but I had to restate my hypothesis again in my mind. I had honored Nathanael's would-be birthday year after year on 11/11. *Was it possible that when I finally let go in 2009, God was gently reminding me that the baby was okay, that my baby was in heaven?*

As I pulled into the parking lot of my office building, I felt lighter and perhaps a little less lonely, and heaven didn't seem so far away. What should have been the easiest anniversary so far, as an eighteen-year veteran of Veterans Day, had been the turning point I desperately needed. *Perhaps, after all these years of going to the pond, God thought I didn't need training wheels anymore.* I grabbed my jacket, and before leaving the safety of my car, I whispered a quiet and belated "Happy Birthday" to an invisible angel who I hoped would continue to visit me nightly at 11:11.

CHAPTER 21:

THE ENEMY OF MY SLEEP

(2018)

How I wish that was the end of it. We were going through a great deal of stress at the time, and because of my health, I had walked away from a lucrative job offer with a large medical institution that was recruiting me back to Human Resources with a specialization in corporate employee benefits. Garrett was traveling across the country every other week. One morning on the way to a weekly physical therapy session, I listened to a beautiful song that I had been playing on continuous loop for weeks. It was dark outside, and my headlights made the sides of the frozen road look like diamonds in the light. Instead of singing along, I listened intently to the words and its message about Jesus making us clean, clean from every kind of sin, and it ministered to my heart as I cried on the straightaway to work.

Great! I don't have time to fix my makeup in the parking lot before I walk in, I fussed as I rummaged around the front seat for the box of tissue.

I didn't know if God spoke to my spirit or not, but something inside me realized these tears were old and musty and stored up like plaque in the arteries. The song so beautifully illustrated how we can be made clean from our shame, and it hit me that shame was the obstacle that had delayed the progress of my grief. The Bible made it clear that I was forgiven for all sins when I repented. I was to walk in freedom from these shameful feelings, even if I had conviction that my abortion was a wrong choice. As I used the rearview mirror and a tissue to blend what remained of my makeup, I knew God and I had already been over the topic of shame a thousand times. I sat in the car intentionally silent to remember that Christ died for me. God had long since forgiven me for the abortion. The person who wasn't letting me off the hook was me!

The 11:11 clock sitings happened so regularly that they evolved from quirky to concerning. Seeing that time on the clock stopped making me smile and began to trigger thoughts about the abortion, thoughts peppered with dark questions. *What did it really mean?* One night, alone and fighting through a terrible migraine attack, I padded out to a file cabinet in the garage in stocking feet and walked slowly to a bulging hanging file stuffed with stapled packets of papers. I had looked through it earlier that year when doing some research on the abortion, but this time I knew what I was searching for. I felt powerless to walk away from the morbid curiosity of looking through this file of obstetrical medical records from 2000-2001. I fell onto the couch, tucking my feet under me. I meticulously scanned each page, taking care to check dates and document titles until I came to a yellow carbon copy surgical consent form. I winced upon seeing my own signature, inarguable evidence that at least mentally I appeared to know what I was doing when I authorized the doctor to arrest my baby's life. I don't know what possessed me to run my finger along the curves of my name until I pressed hard on the condemning paper in an effort to erase it, to at least smudge it so that no one could see what I had done.

The operative report felt like it stared up at me as I stared down at it. I read the names of the anesthesiologist and nurse anesthetist and the OR nurse who attended the surgery along with my OB-GYN. I felt ashamed to think that they were present for the darkest moment of my life, and I hoped they'd never remember me among the countless women they had attended. I read about the surgical supplies they used, the kind of anesthesia administered, and how they had noted my vitals before and after the administration of propofol, but I wasn't prepared to look further down the page to find the darkness of what I had suspected.

ANESTHESIA ADMINISTERED: 10:58 a.m.

PROCEDURE START TIME: 11:03 a.m.

PROCEDURE END TIME: 11:35 a.m.

A kinder me would have never looked this up. A kinder me would have never—Jesus would have never—but I was not free from the talons of the enemy. In a matter of minutes, the enemy had come for a visit to defile the meaningful 11:11 anniversary memorial for my sweet baby. There in my lap was the medical record that quickened the pounding of the migraine in my head, the surgical record that candidly stated the facts of what had happened during my abortion surgery. Nathanael was due on 11/11/2000. It was clear that he had likely died at 11:11 a.m. on that fateful day.

That night I did a little journaling, ever the perpetual insomniac. I was so exhausted that I dropped into bed at 9:30 p.m. I woke up when Garrett came home at 10:45, but thankfully I fell back to sleep without the usual angst. I never dreamed specifically about Natty, other than vague dreams of being pregnant or tending to someone else's baby, sometimes a foster child, but these wonderful maternal dreams only happened once or twice a year. As I slept, a night terror played out in vivid detail, like a video of the events of 2000, which built to a dramatic scene in a hospital recovery room where I was hysterical. I felt like I was drowning and wrestled to wake up in an anxious state of sleep paralysis. I tried to scream in an attempt to exit the dream, but no words came out. The plexiglass at the surface of my dream state broke, and I sat up in bed gasping, realizing I was having night sweats, and I stared into the darkness of our bedroom. I felt confused and too scared to move, yet I wanted desperately to go back to sleep, to alter the course of my dream, to stop the abortion, to give birth to him—if only to meet him for a minute.

As rational thought returned, I forced myself to get up for a dry t-shirt, and as I stopped on the way to my closet, I made the mistake of looking at my alarm clock to see if it was early morning, my usual time to dream. The clock startled me, and I froze, my feet firmly planted on the carpet. It was 11:11 p.m. Things were often worse at night, and knowing that, I pushed through the rush of adrenaline, went to the bathroom, and refilled my water glass, half believing that water would make it better as I'd so often told my daughter when she would wake up in the night. I gave the water a little power of its own by washing down a second Tylenol PM and I quietly rifled through the nightstand drawer for my headphones to put on a Bible podcast and try to make it all go away. I settled my shoulder into the mattress, trying to adjust my pillow without waking Garrett, and I slowly pulled the down coverlet over my exposed shoulder. I closed my eyes and tried to get a deep breath, as my confiding pillow soaked up silent tears.

Another sip of water or a trip to the bathroom wasn't going to calm the roar that began to build in my stomach and throat. I crept downstairs and plopped down on the cold leather sofa and stared at the shadows on the window in front of me. Prayer poured out of my exhausted mind.

"You've always been there, God. I know You don't endorse numerology or humans ascribing meaning to unmeaningful things, but I want to accept 11:11 as a gift from You, Lord, whether it makes sense to anyone else or not." I realized I was praying into the dark, alone in our living room, as I talked this out in an effort to understand this newfound revelation.

I come in the name of Christ Jesus against the enemy, who has tried to terrorize me with 11:11 on the clock, as if it is something from a horror movie. Even if my baby died at 11:11, the enemy meant to scare me with dark and agonizing thoughts of how he left this world. But tonight, I claim that his death at 11:11 was a resurrection and his safe delivery back to You, God. It should have been his earthly birthday, but 11:11 was also his eternal birthday, and I thank You, God, for being there with me on that dark day, never letting go of my hand, never leaving my side, and receiving my baby into Your care. I dropped my head, emotionally exhausted.

Thank You for being with me at all times and especially on Natty's birthday at the pond. Every year I go there to honor Your faithfulness, God, and to honor my son who died in a way I will forever regret. When I notice 11:11 on a clock, I will receive it as a free gift from you, Father, a reminder of Your forgiveness to me, and a reminder to forgive myself. I will take it as assurance that Nathanael is fully restored and with You in heaven. I'm sorry, Lord, that it took so great a tragedy to break the chains of my pride and shame and to finally submit to You as my Creator and my Savior.

When I invited Jesus into the darkness with me and admitted my fear and shortcomings, He was faithful to shine His healing light upon me, and the demons had to flee. My Savior was bigger than my biggest demon. He overcame the grave for me and for all. "O death, where is thy sting?" (1 Corinthians 15:55 [KJV])

A friend in the ministry of abortion healing, Karen A. Ellison, has said,

"Bringing things into the light is only profitable when it is redemptive." Many people would find it neither redemptive nor healthy to review medical records surrounding the most traumatic year of a person's life, but for me, it took the ugliest truth in black and white on yellow paper to reach the end of my sorrow. I had to face the full extent of my horror in the darkest valley before I could look up to see there was light. With the shackles unhinged from my ankles, I was gaining freedom from the primary obstacle that hindered the deepening of my faith—shame. I had made my peace with God, and my heart felt ready to reach out for what I was starving for—connection.

CHAPTER 22:

CONNECTION

(2019)

After New Year's I came down with an annual cold. Getting sick gave me an opportunity to involuntarily rest, as I didn't have the energy to work on the long list of productive administrative tasks I needed to do. I had run out of excuses to keep ignoring the book I'd not yet finished called *Surrendering the Secret* by Pat Layton. I had started the book but abandoned it after two chapters, emotionally unprepared at the time. I had forgotten that it was more of a Bible study than a book, meant to be completed in a group setting along with video sessions. The book had traveled with me on a plane trip to Southern California in a sincere effort to start reading it on the plane, but I'd also wanted to challenge myself to no longer hide a book like this—this book which had the word *abortion* in the subtitle. I thought about pulling it out during my outbound flight, but the tiny word *abortion* felt like it was printed in 40-point font, and I was sure that someone in row 22B would be able to read my book from where I sat in 7D. It was a busy trip, so I only cracked the spine of the book and re-read the introduction.

Back at home, I set up a TV tray next to my sick bed and began to watch the online video sessions that accompanied the book. Fueled by my Type A personality, I watched all eight videos in one day. I could argue that they were fairly short, but the author intended the videos to be consumed at most once a week. I rationalized my binge approach by promising myself I would watch the videos again later after I'd completed the corresponding homework in the book. As I listened to the women in the video series share about their abortion experiences, their stories transformed into inspiring testimonies, and I wanted to see how the curriculum came together. I could say my approach was merely academic, but I knew that as I watched the video, I was longing for connection—connection to other women, connection to other mothers. I had lived on the island of secrecy and shame for nineteen years, and these women I voluntarily invited into my laptop, surrounded by cough drops and Kleenex, made me feel less alone for the first time in nearly two decades. I assumed being honest with anyone about my abortion loss would result in being abandoned on a true island of isolation, because everyone would turn their backs on me. I had let the enemy of my soul convince me that revealing my secret would be my demise. This book, *Surrendering the Secret*, helped me finally understand that if I lay my secret down, I would feel lighter, and perhaps my muscles would stop aching. Most importantly, I would have two hands free to love myself and others.

Garrett and I were in a major life transition moving from a rental property back to our family home, and it was the first season I had spent away from hosting a small group Bible study. I knew that staying isolated and only working through a personal study that winter was not enough connection. I signed up for a home-based Bible study where I wasn't the hostess, and it was a comfortable fit. I immediately hit it off with the women in the group, but there were afternoons I could feel heat rising around the edges of my face, as if my head was wrapped in papier-mâché. It was the strangest feeling—often easy to ignore during the times of laughter shared over food and fellowship between our group of women. When I was listening intently, I felt focused and clear, but other times when I would laugh or smile at the ladies who were fast becoming friends, this premonitory feeling would sneak up on me, much like the aura of a migraine. Smiling amplified this aura that felt like the pull of a facial mask tugging and cracking as it dried across my cheeks. In spite of this, I was having a genuinely fun time with these ladies, some of whom I knew from church and three others who were new acquaintances.

One afternoon, Joanne was sharing about a painful experience. I was drawn quickly and deeply into her story, and I squirmed in my seat to shift chronic pain from one side of my hip to the other. The emotion visible on her face as she shared so vulnerably led me to empathize with her pain. She cried, the ladies in our group cried, we prayed. We extended the time allotted for our study group to allow the time and space for the Holy Spirit to achieve healing and victory over an area of pain in her life that day.

I had shared with my Bible cohorts that I was dealing with some debilitating health issues. Most notable at the time were daily chronic migraines and painful light sensitivity, rheumatoid arthritis, and several frustrating complications of thyroid cancer surgery. One afternoon at Bible study, as I shared the couch with one of the women who was fast becoming a friend, I reached up to tug at my neck and shoulder. Immediately my couch mate leapt into action and put her warm hand on my burning shoulder. She began to pray for me quietly, and before I could thank her and reposition myself, the women surrounded me on all sides. There was nowhere to go to escape, and my face felt unbearably hot. I'd grown to love these friends enough that I felt willing to be more vulnerable, and I began to let the mask of cheer and chronic smiles slide down my face like a melted popsicle. I was not new to the evangelical Christian experience, and I knew that as the women got up one by one and filed over to where I was sitting, it meant only one thing. They were going to pray over me, whether I liked it or not.

Time slowed down, and anxiety began to bubble up and press against my sternum, with the distinct outline of a large, familiar fist. I tried to summon the additional maturity I hoped came with being over forty, in an effort to keep myself glued to my seat.

You can do this, I silently encouraged myself like some kind of internal Jiminy Cricket. I had learned to be a fighter, but fleeing was still what I did best when things became scary. This time I felt anchored to the couch beneath my thighs, almost paralyzed as I watched these beautiful women move into structured slowness. I felt mesmerized the way I did as a kid watching thick ketchup slowly descend along the side of a bottle until a strong hit to the side broke it free into an unexpected thud on a waiting plate. I wasn't interested in being struck with a hard blow, physically or spiritually, and I had no plans to expel my contents anywhere or to anyone. I was in control of my waterworks, and perhaps it was time for me to bolt. Three women were behind me, one was to my left, and two were on my right. My only visible exit was the front door straight ahead, and since it's customary to remove shoes in the rainy Northwest, making a run for it wasn't a feasible option. I had felt safe talking about simple things, easy things, their things.

How did this happen?

Compassion was something I poured out onto others, but my well was entirely dry. My grandma and my mom passed down a "pull yourself up by your bootstraps" mentality that had helped me achieve a list of titles, awards, and designations that no longer inspired me. This fierce independence had served me well in the business world but had left my body like a horse put out to pasture far too young.

I had prayed for and even laid hands on other women in a Bible study setting before, but my preference was to be the giver and not the receiver. If someone said, "I'll pray for you" at the end of a coffee date, I accepted it and was sincerely thankful. The expression "prayers up" on social media was even better—removed, less intimate, safe. Praying in groups, what we called "corporate prayer," was my specialty. Somehow in the anonymity of a large group where prayers were meant to be a broad paintbrush, my love of stringing together powerful and moving words to lift people up felt natural. I knew what my hang-ups were with intimate prayer. I'd done some reflection on it, I'd prayed about the issue dozens of times, and I'd even worked on it in counseling. I chalked up part of my discomfort with intimate prayer to a personal space issue. A sort of heebie-jeebie feeling was my regular companion when people got too close to my body, let alone when anyone other than my husband touched me. It was a secret and well-disguised problem, because I would sweat and smile to spare anyone's feelings rather than speak up for my own social comfort. "What if" thinking was like a whirlpool in my head.

What if my stomach growled in a quiet room while someone was praying? What if my nose ran while my head was bowed in prayer, or, worse yet, what if my nose dripped on my lap for lack of a tissue? Worst of all, what if I lost control of my feelings in public?

Before I had time to make a run for the door with a lame excuse like a forgotten appointment or an unexpected bout of diarrhea, these women had already set about their work. They were praying, and it was time for me to quell the racing thoughts of panic and pride.

I welcomed their love and intercessory prayers for pain relief, but I'd have to hunker down and ride out the discomfort of my invisible mask that was now palpably lifting up around my chin and jowls. I closed my eyes and bowed my head because that's just what I did, and I'd been doing it all of my life. It was also to show reverence and genuine respect for my friends. I breathed in through my nose and only released my exhalation one bit at a time, concerned that my breath would not be fresh at this time of day. Breathing calmly, letting my abdomen relax and expand, was impossible for me, so I turned to a breath prayer, breathing in and out along with the slow, measured recitation of J-E-S-U-S as my metronome.

These women aren't judging you. I began to let my breath come naturally, almost involuntarily, as I dropped my shoulders and realized that if I got out of my anxious head, I could feel the warmth of their individual hands on my shoulders, my neck, my back, and my head.

A sense of holiness came over me like a gentle fog, neither warm nor cold. Anxiety began to be displaced by peace, and I sensed that I was sharing in a sacred moment, what I imagined might be something like entering into the very throne room of God. He was a gentle gardener, pruning me in the right season. He never pushed me too far in my walk. He brought me to this place and to this day, as these women enveloped me on all sides, just when I was broken enough to receive their gifts of insight and healing. There was nowhere to go and nothing to do but to let go. I took another deep breath and asked myself,

What's the worst thing that could happen? I imagined I might cry. I didn't know all of these women well, but over the years countless women had cried in front of me during times of prayer, and I never judged any of them. I'd been the first one to jump up to find a box of tissue or pull out a clean-but-crumpled napkin from my purse to give them. In my work life, everyone came to me with their problems in confidence because I could be trusted.

Why is it okay for everybody else to break down, but I rarely let myself be vulnerable?

There was no stopping what was happening, as these prayer warriors were steadfastly on the task of moving through a supernatural agenda to which I was not privy. I listened to their individual and collective voices and let myself begin to float. I started with what I knew best and what was most comfortable—I prayed for each woman in my head. I invited the Holy Spirit to come, though He'd apparently already invited Himself here before my car had pulled into the driveway. My anxious spirit became still and the racing thoughts in my head stopped. I could hear the voices of two women I knew on my right. One prayed in a tongue I could not recognize. Another spoke in English mixed with a prayer language. It didn't matter that I didn't understand what they were saying. I believed and accepted that they were speaking in commune with God and that something holy was happening.

To the left, my newest friend, Joanne, was praying in English, and I understood that she was praying deeply for my heart. Behind me, there were the most gentle and delicate hands upon my neck. There was a feeling of warm light and comfort coming against my pain. The woman touching my neck prayed with a mix of song and soft prayer. It was as if she spoke in

Hebrew, and my mind began to drift into imagery, seeing her in a faraway land. She was no longer the friend I knew from town; she had taken on another persona for me. I felt transported to an ancient land, to the place of Christ's wanderings. I felt a momentary distraction from the usual companions of my mind—rationalization and anxiety, and I fought to silence them again. It was not the first time I had felt a palpable enemy who wanted to keep me from healing prayer and this kind of connection. My foe, the devil, preferred me to limp through life with a bear trap snapped shut around my ankles. Tears came to my eyes, as I allowed tightly held emotions to move in me, letting go of the fear and the need to be in control. I took another breath just as Joanne began speaking.

"Lord, I feel the heaviness of my sister. Help her as she goes with you deep into her feelings of grief."

Grief? How did she know I carried grief? I hadn't shared anything about grief or loss with this new group of ladies. She had no way of knowing.

Floodgates of pain opened up in me, and I began to weep. It wasn't an ugly cry, but I didn't stop the tears as they rolled over the edge of my lower lids. The voice of the gentle woman of ancient days singing behind me was comforting to my heart. My mind could not comprehend it all, but my spirit felt as if it was being washed with the warmth of anointing oils. I felt heavy, as if I could faint or sink into the chair. I kept my eyes closed, as I became more aware of the holy harmony of the women praying together. I heard Joanne break into cries. My heart became heavy for her, and I wanted to take her hand. I was touched that she seemed to be crying in empathy and compassion for me.

She was praying over me as if she could feel the grief she spoke of, when all of a sudden, she cried out,

"I see a baby," and with a gasp she added, "The most beautiful baby!"

My throat let go of a choking sound followed by quiet tears, as I hovered between supernatural revelation and the shock that a woman I met only months before could know any details at the center of my heart's greatest pain. I cried out in her praying, and she continued to share that this baby was so beautiful and that she could see the baby with Jesus. In that moment pain ran through my body like a searing wave of chills up my back. It felt as if God had spoken to me directly, personally, with things that only He could know. The women began to pray with greater fervor, as if they were picking up the pieces of the heavy weight I shed.

"This baby—this baby is just so beautiful. He has the biggest cheeks and so much hair!"

I cried out. "What?" You can't know that. My daughter had the biggest cheeks of any baby I've ever seen and was born with a full head of hair." I opened my eyes and reached for the box of tissues.

This couldn't be happening. This was something that happened in movies or at some kind of teenage séance, but it wasn't scary at all. I released myself to cry with abandon, and there was no holding back. *How could she have known about the baby? How could she have known he was a boy? How could she have known descriptive details that were unique to his sister?*

What had I done to deserve this unplanned, unscripted, powerful assurance from God? I felt an unexplainable sense of release that I didn't think was possible because of what I ascribed to be the unforgiveable nature of my sin. Finally, today was an audible answer to the question I asked God every fall at a watery gravesite—all the times I asked God if Nathanael was at peace. Through the vision of another believer, He answered bigger than I could ever have imagined. It felt solid, and I felt sure—sure for the first time that I would not only see my son again in heaven, but that he was safe, and he was treasured.

For years I had been asking the Lord to forgive the circumstances surrounding the death of the baby I wanted with all my heart. For many years I had looked up into the trees around the pond where I'd scattered his ashes and told my son how sorry I was for what happened. And every year I stood there waiting for a breeze to come up through the trees for some kind of acknowledgement, as if he would say, "It's okay, Mama. I forgive you."

As I drove home, I replayed what happened over and over again, allowing the repetition to etch deep grooves in my memory. It was like a morning dream from which I didn't want to wake up, and I tried desperately to go back to sleep to see how it ended. I wanted more. I just wanted more.

A few weeks later at Bible study, we enjoyed our usual snacking, prayer, and discussion of the scripture we were dissecting. Amidst our Bibles and dessert plates was a beautiful paper-covered box with a sheer ribbon tied loosely around it. When it was time to go, I began stuffing papers into my Bible cover and collecting loose pens and highlighters, and I got up to put my shoes on by the door.

"Wait!" Joanne called out to me. "You can't go yet," and she patted the seat cushion of the chair I had just left behind.

"Come sit."

I scanned the faces of the other ladies, and it appeared they knew something.

Her enthusiasm was nearly unbridled as she stood up to get the elegant box from the coffee table and bent over at the waist to present it to me like a ballerina executing a pose.

"This is for me? Oh, my gracious, what did you do?"

Joanne was a gifted artist, and the week before I had seen posts of her work on social media. We had recently enjoyed lunch in her garden, the highlight of which for me was seeing her cozy and well-appointed artist's studio. I pulled the ribbon loose on the box, taking care to twirl it into a spool in my hands to express my intention to keep it.

"What a beautiful box," I complimented, as I opened the magnetic paperboard lid to see there was no gift tissue in it, but rather piece of elegant metallic tulle enshrouding what looked like a painting.

I gasped with excitement, "Did you paint something for me?"

Joanne's face scrunched up with a mix of mischievousness and a forceful attempt not to cry. I immediately knew what it was, as I pulled back the fabric. There inside the box, I saw the face of an angel—a baby with blue-green eyes that sparkled in a knowing smile, ample loose curls of light amber hair with streaks of black and gold, and plump, round cheeks.

"Joanne. It's him!" And indeed, it could only be my sweet baby, my Nathanael. In her heartfelt effort to portray the baby she had seen in her vision, she had painted a baby whose face miraculously bore a slight resemblance to my daughter at the same age. Joanne had never seen a photo of my Lily.

"He looks a bit like his sister. How is this possible?"

I looked up to find that all of the ladies were crying, and some were clasping their hands together with amazement and joy.

This ethereal painting holds a revered spot among my many treasures. It felt impossible to adequately thank someone for giving me the gift of seeing the baby I wish more than anything I could have held, if only for a little while. I know I will see him again in eternity. Not a moment before I was ready, God commissioned a painter to grab hold of a piece of heaven and pull it down to earth for me.

All these years, I thought I'd been so courageous in facing my grief. I thought I had read all the books, done all the right things, performed every ritual. I wrote countless poems, went to God with a repentant heart ritualistically over and over, but I had let pride get in the way of hearing from God. I had let the shame of sharing my story keep healing from my soul. I had let the possibility of embarrassment prevent others from laying hands on me, and I'd kept the fear of losing control of my feelings in front of others rob me of the possibility of feeling something other than grief for the first time since that dark day. I had placed a stumbling block in the gap where Jesus belonged and unintentionally blocked the best gift that only God could dream up—for an artist to unmistakably see my son, to paint him from memory and present him to me in a beautiful box, lavishly wrapped with the signature of God.

Photo Credit to Jody Ashley Perkins

CHAPTER 23:

REGRET

(2019)

As I continued to meet other women through a variety of church functions, I had the honor of connecting with many young moms who seemed to have it all together. I met women with small children who worked both inside and outside of the home and were busy driving kids from one event to another, balancing it all with some kind of inner joy that was foreign to me when I was a young mom. My new friends had ups and downs common to all people, but it was evident that they were somehow juggling the craziness proactively, and from a strong foundation—a rock more reliable than their own intestinal fortitude. Even in my 40s with two grown children, my kind of crazy always felt reactive, like something that had to be managed.

With a keen perspective, Karen A. Ellison wrote in her book, *Healing the Hurt that Won't Heal*: "A life that's not built on God's will and His truth is not a place of freedom, but a place that always needs to be managed." After a lifetime of captivity and reactivity, my attempts at self-management had exhausted me.

One night when I was too exhausted to sleep, as the dark hours stretched out before me, my husband slept peacefully, while I felt insomnia winning and anxiety creeping in. I didn't have a gift of hearing audibly from God, but that night I distinctly heard Him speak to my spirit the words,

"Tell your story."

I opened my eyes to reorient myself in our dark bedroom, focusing on the barely perceptible light from the thin slits between the window blinds.

What?

"Tell your story," I heard the voice again.

God, is that you? A dialogue began in my racing mind.

Tell my story. What? If that was God, does He mean I should finally dust off my half-written novel? I realized it probably wasn't God endorsing a provocative story I had begun writing in 2011.

Okay, maybe it's a blog article or one of my short stories He wants me to develop?

Knowing sleep would be impossible, I got up to refill my water bottle, washing it down with my nightly elixir of sleep aids.

I gathered my pillow and my favorite wool Pendleton and trudged off to the guest room in the dark, the well-worn path in the carpet was a trustworthy trail. I tossed the ballet company of throw pillows onto the floor and climbed into the smell of clean sheets, aggressively adjusting my pillow. I took a few deep breaths, but this bedroom was in the front of the house and it was beginning to lighten with the coming of dawn. Sleep remained elusive. Two decades of sleeplessness had taught me that endlessly lying there was a bad idea and as I reached for my cell phone to find a podcast on my favorite app, a thought flashed through my mind with force.

Tell THE story.

Sitting up in a wave of fear, I didn't care that I needed to speak out loud into the privacy of the room.

"Tell the story. Tell THE story." I muttered.

Oh, God. You want me to write THAT story? Really, God? I can't do that.

Natty's story. You want me to write about the abortion? Are you serious?

I sat frozen, afraid to breathe, scared to make a sound. I thought if I was quiet enough God might speak again to say He was kidding or that

He might send some kind of sign to let me off the hook. I startled at the sound of the neighbor's Harley-Davison motorcycle firing up, signaling that it was 4:40 a.m. I flopped back onto the bed, my head hitting the cold pillow a little too hard.

Anything but that story, God. Please? I pleaded like the spoiled child who lived in my head.

I knew the dialogue I put forward in that cold and dark morning was solely for my own benefit. Over the coming weeks I searched for any practical excuses I could find, justifying putting off writing a book due to a myriad of health issues, several of which prevented me from being able to work on a computer at all. Chronic daily migraines limited me with blurred vision every afternoon and evening, and rheumatoid arthritis was taking a toll on my hands, elbows, shoulders and ankles. Insomnia, anxiety, and gastrointestinal issues regularly made sleep impossible. My ability to focus on a single task and see it through to completion was a regular impossibility. I was perplexed that God would ask me to do this in my darkest season of medical depression, but I knew that if He wanted me to write it, it would be to help and bless others. It hadn't entered my mind that God could use the writing of a manuscript to finish a healing work in me.

One of the many beauties of writing was that I could speak my whole truth. Unless a reader puts the book down or ultimately tossed it into a box to donate to a rummage sale, there was no stopping me as a writer. Once I accepted God's challenge, there was no turning back, no matter the obstacles. One of my favorite quotes by P.D. James, a British mystery novelist, declares, "Nothing that happens to a writer—however happy, however tragic—is ever wasted." I believed in the truth of this quote in the marrow of my bones.

The confidence I mustered behind a keyboard quickly slipped into the shadows when I was faced with the eyes of a real person. I memorized my elevator speech about the loss of my second pregnancy in case I was ever pushed to answer, and I assumed people would stop listening if I was honest. My explanation was polished, short, and politically correct. It made the listener feel comfortable with an uncomfortable topic.

I lived daily with the medical complications of my traumatic abortion surgeries, but on this side of heaven I struggled to make peace with the agony of the greatest regret of my life—the regret of not seeing my pregnancy through to the end. If I had waited one more week, my OB-GYN said, "we would have to make you deliver the fetus." He said this option was more traumatic for most mothers than the proposed surgical D&E during which I would be completely asleep under general anesthesia and would "not remember anything." At the time, I couldn't imagine anything more terrifying or heartbreaking than being induced into labor for an unknown number of hours, only to deliver my son lifeless and blue. I couldn't bear to ask if they would have taken him away or if they would have let me hold him, wrapped in a blanket far too big. They never explained what termination would look like if I had chosen to wait until the next week. They only referred to it once as "induction and labor." In our state of shock and disbelief, it made sense to take the seemingly easier surgical option.

I was induced at full term with my daughter, and I wondered if delivering my baby boy would have been similar. My mind could only grasp that he would not be viable to deliver at seventeen to eighteen weeks. It wasn't until writing my story that I finally gathered the courage to look up what they meant by their one-time mention of induction and delivery. Second trimester abortion was closely tied to the words "partial-birth abortion" in online searches, and because that was such a highly politicized term, I thought it certainly didn't apply to me. I sat speechless at the computer monitor, unable to process that my story not only grazed the topic of partial-birth abortion, but it had been right in the middle of it, before it was banned in 2003. The Partial-Birth Abortion Ban Act of 2003 amended the federal criminal code to prohibit any physician from knowingly performing the procedure except when necessary to save the life of the mother.[8] I began to wonder if the medical center staff hadn't given us the option to deliver our baby via medical induction because it was motivated by insurance coverage and might be less litigious for the hospital and the doctor.

Going to sleep for the surgery on the worst day of my life seemed like it would be less traumatic. However, as I connected with women who had chosen to deliver their babies with poor fetal prognosis or who had died in-utero, I couldn't help but want what they'd had – the chance to hold their intact baby, no matter how traumatic and tragic. I could have seen my son, even if it was a gruesome picture to others. I could have held my baby, gently traced the outlines of his immeasurably tiny fingers and toes, imagined how his unnaturally small face might have later changed into features I recognized in my husband, myself, or perhaps my daughter.

It was months before I could muster the courage to further investigate the differences between the two options of medical termination we were given in 2000. I read a medical article that detailed how they would have inserted a needle into my abdomen to inject potassium chloride or digoxin directly into the heart of the fetus to stop it from beating. Other articles detailed that at nineteen weeks a solution of saline or urea would have been injected into the amniotic sac to soften the fetal bones.[9] When I read those words, I pushed away from my computer in disgust and hurried to the bathroom with the urge to vomit. But later that night I forced myself to continue reading, because I suspected that facing the facts surrounding how my son was killed, no matter how brutal, might have held a piece of my healing. I learned that after this lethal injection, I would have then been induced to go into labor to deliver an incredibly tiny and dead baby. In my grieved imagination, I'd somehow thought that if he was delivered intact, he could have lived long enough for me to hold him while he slipped away. One of my regrets was thinking that I should have perhaps forgone the amnesia of anesthesia in the hopes that labor and delivery might have been less painful for the baby. These injectable medications are likely used to decrease the risk of a premature live birth. I found no evidence in my surgical notes that the baby's heart was stopped before the abortion procedure, which further compounded the trauma in my mind. When I steeled myself to read the description of the surgical D&E process in my own medical records, I pressed my cheek flat against my desk and cried until I soaked the quilted placemat. It took nineteen years for me to finally have the courage to read that forceps were used to collapse his skull, killing the baby, and making it easier for Dr. Parr to remove the arms and legs and body parts. I felt like a wood-fired stake was driven into my heart—searing and scarring it, branding my heart forever with the word regret.

I will forever regret accepting the hospital staff's recommendation that we terminate our pregnancy by second trimester surgical D&E, not leaving our baby "intact." They didn't use these words, and perhaps if they had, I might have asked more questions. I wish that we'd let nature take its course over our pregnancy, and I could have carried our son to term for as long as he might have lived.

I knew my dreams were a way for my mind and heart to process and integrate the trauma, but vivid flashbacks during my waking hours were never a welcome visitor. At times, memories played like vibrant full-color video clips in my mind, and they triggered powerful and unexpected emotions. Sometimes I could identify what triggered a flashback—a song, a social media post on a neonatal loss support group—but other times it came like a shocking slap across the face. I worked hard to have myself together on the outside, but there were days I was a roaring inferno on the inside. I walked around with a hard shell on the outside that held back a melted mess in the middle, especially when heat was applied.

Our abortion choice that day canceled all our other choices, and because of that I will never know if our baby could have been miraculously healed in the womb if carried further into the pregnancy. If he had survived to a gestational age of viability and was delivered alive, would he have been rushed off to surgery, or would he have lived for only a few minutes or a few hours? The story of our baby treads upon the lines between pro-choice and pro-life positions because many people can see both sides of our agonizing decision. I can only speak from my personal experience of abortion, but I know that if a woman comes to me deliberating whether or not to choose abortion, I will answer every question she has with uncensored honesty and empathy. I don't have an agenda, but I do have a hope—a hope that one less woman can avoid being left as I was, broken and forever changed. In sharing my story with a deliberating woman or family, I pray it might help them thoughtfully consider the ramifications of abortion. I wish I had closed my ears to the disinterested medical professionals involved in my son's case and left the fate of our baby to the heart and hands of God. I wish I had made my decision differently with the wisdom of hindsight and a strong and developed faith. With all that I am, I believe that carrying Nathanael to term would have been the most "compassionate choice" for my son and for me.

Whatever the outcome for my sweet infant, I could have said that I gave him a safe place to fight for his life. I would have created the time and space for a miracle. Perhaps he would have been born healed of his afflictions. Perhaps he would have been born and exceeded all restorative surgical expectations following his birth. Even if he had been born with a beautiful cry of life that only lasted a few minutes, any time to hold him would have been meaningful and treasured.

I have been honored to hear the stories of parents who have suffered neonatal and infant loss through national and international online support groups. When I see their beautiful photographs of tiny baby feet, knit caps, and handprints, I grieve with them, I pray for them, and in the privacy of my heart, I long for similar pictures or mementos. Most cultures create space for the viewing of a body after death for the vital reason that it can make the abstract absence of a loved one concrete for the grief-torn mind. My grief process might have been shorter, less jagged, and inherently different had I been able to say goodbye to a physical baby rather than to an imaginary construct of dreams and a tiny urn of ashes.

The simultaneous grief and comfort I see in the faces of mothers and parents who get to hold their infants before saying goodbye always bring the pain of empathy to my chest. If the only picture of Nathanael seemed too raw for the camera, I still wanted that for myself. I could have lovingly wrapped his unnaturally tiny frame in a blanket, with the dignity that every life deserves. I live with the regret of not being able to memorize the features of his developing face, the outline of his lips, the furrow of his brow, or the wrinkles on his tiny feet. I regret not giving him a chance to try, a chance to fight, a chance to cry for his parents—to be comforted and to feel love the way it can be felt without words. I would give anything to buy back the opportunity to say goodbye or to say hello to Nathanael for however long God intended.

As I continued my research, I ran across a concept I had never heard of, an option that that gives families a meaningful alternative to medically advised abortion. I read the illuminated lines on my laptop monitor in stunned silence as I learned about a specialized branch of hospice care called perinatal hospice. I read and I cried, unable to tear myself away from my laptop to get tissue, as I began to imagine how different my son's passing might have been if we had known about this option at the time of our devastating perinatal diagnosis. I was somewhat relieved to learn that it came about in 1996, and it was likely not yet available at our hospital. Perinatal hospice has also been called "hospice in the womb," providing support as early as the time of diagnosis.[10] Hospice services can step in to help expecting parents with emotional support, planning the birth experience, and preliminary medical decision-making before the baby is born. If the baby survives the delivery process, hospice can provide palliative care if the child lives for a few minutes, hours, or days. They provide essential newborn care through warmth, comfort, nutrition, and medical treatments to improve the baby's level of comfort. If at any time the child's medical condition improves—a true miracle in these situations—traditional medical care can become involved again in the hopes of saving or extending the baby's life. The perinatal hospice approach supports families from diagnosis through the end of the pregnancy and provides vital grief support and resources. These compassionate and trained providers can also assist the family with making plans after the baby's death ranging from photography to how to handle the baby's remains, as well as providing ideas for memorializing the baby to acknowledge that the child was real.

CHAPTER 24:

ONIONS

(2019)

Iread about perinatal hospice for several hours, reviewing websites and watching touching and inspirational video testimonies. Emotionally exhausted, I stared out the window like a dazed and distracted child. I pulled out my steno notebook to jot down some names of organizations rendering perinatal hospice in the U.S., finding my last journal entry which illustrated a crude drawing of onions and their tightly stacked layers as a metaphor for the many layers of grief. Distracted by my sketch, I typed the word onion into my web browser. I was immediately gratified by hundreds of pictures of onion cells of every variety shown under microscopy, and they were beautiful.

The pictures led to articles that boasted of the health benefits of onions providing vitamins, minerals, fiber, and beta-carotene for a healthy metabolism, and said that onions are also high in folate (folic acid).[11] Folic acid is a vital supplement, especially during pregnancy, and has been implicated in the prevention of neural tube birth defects. I learned that the ancient Egyptians even worshipped onions because of their concentric circles symbolizing eternity. I had always been fascinated by plants with patterns, such as onions and grapefruits. For me, these beautiful foods were clear evidence of a divine Creator.

Why do onions make us cry? Apparently, the chemical irritant known as syn-Propanethial-S-oxide stimulates our eyes' lachrymal glands to release tears.[12] I have tried various ways to cut onions to avoid tearing up by refrigerating them first or using a food processor. Someone told me once to try wearing swim goggles. One blog recommended chewing gum while chopping onions to help breathe through the mouth, better dispersing the eye irritant. People are by nature pleasure-seeking and pain-avoiding. My study of the onion pointed back to my own character, my own techniques for avoidance. I tried to be a grief prodigy in the early years, but distraction and avoidance of pain became my real area of mastery.

I ran across more images of what I thought were onion circles under x-ray exposure. I'd never seen anything quite so beautiful, even though the images were black and white. I squinted to read the small font and was surprised to see that these were no longer slides of onion cells at high magnification, but they were images of tear drops under the microscope, and they were exquisite. Delicate and patterned like a snowflake or the infinite combinations of frost on a windshield, I was drawn into the beauty. My internet browser helped me drill down into the chemistry and structure of tear drops, and my heart did a flip-flop in my chest as I read that every tear is unique, like a fingerprint. Tears are also different depending on whether they are caused by physical pain (reflex tears), a chemical reaction (basal tears), anger, or even grief (emotional tears). Photographer Maurice Mikkers created a beautiful collection of tears in what he calls his "Imaginarium of Tears."[13] Before I knew it, I was fighting back my own tears. How beautiful that these concrete and scientific images mirror the verse found in Psalm 56:8 (NLT) about God catching all of our tears. "You have collected all of my tears in your bottle. You have recorded each one in your book."

God took command of my ADHD and gently but patiently said, "Be still, child." God didn't need me to study onions. He wanted me to meditate on the meaning and value of tears. He wanted me to hear that because every tear is caught and saved by my loving Creator, it was not a waste of time to cry. Crying was not a sign of weakness keeping me from more praiseworthy tasks on my "to do" list. Tears came from feeling viscerally rather than superficially, and yes, tears came from grief.

Grief. For heaven's sake, Lord, haven't I lost enough time on the topic of grief? Was it necessary that I peel back another layer of the proverbial onion in some effort to put the pieces of my story back together in what psychologists call the task of integration and acceptance? Accidental tears were okay, but intentionally touching the place in my heart that hurt felt redundant and unproductive. I imagined that if I could hear God speak, He might have asked me, "Would you prefer to keep wandering in the desert another twenty years?"

I began to realize that I was the one who had chosen to wander, and apparently God knew about it. He'd been with me for every moment of my wandering, and suddenly the years of grief no longer felt wasted, but necessary.

CHAPTER 25:

PERFECTIONISM

(2019)

God asked me to write my story while I was in a deep valley of medical disability, but nineteen years after the tragedy surrounding Nathanael, I had made tremendous progress in dealing with the outcome of my loss, both emotionally and psychologically. Countless hours of reading and counseling had helped me to understand, rationalize, and compartmentalize the trauma in healthy ways. I had made my peace with the dark feelings of regret and guilt, putting them away in tidy metaphorical Tupperware containers so that I could go on with my life. I only took the containers down when I chose to go there in my heart and mind.

Other habits proved harder to break—the deeply ingrained behaviors of double-mindedness and perfectionism. While "perfectionist" was a persona I had readily adopted from childhood, after my unspoken abortion it took tremendous energy to ensure that no one saw the fragility, the shame, and the ugliness I felt on the inside. I was afraid that if I was honest about my second pregnancy, my friends would no longer respect me and would disappear in the night. I'd been such a confident child, but the fear of losing the approval of others—rejection—had become my internal motivation as an adult.

When I went back to church, it initially proved easy for me to pretend I was the definition of a good "church lady." I had put on the protective mask of perfectionism all of my life, not because it was anyone's fault, but because it was all I knew. Perfect was comfortable, safe, and smelled good. Perfect was an efficient operating system. Perfect looked pleasing from the outside and garnered many compliments. More insidious than its societal benefits, however, perfectionism was pretending. It was exhausting, and, if left unchecked, it made me physically sick.

It took half a lifetime of medical appointments and reading to better understand that trying to look perfect on the outside often served to cover up how imperfect things were on the inside. Perfectionism was a family thing, and it was passed down from generation to generation, like dimples, but it wasn't cute. My dimpled daughter was adorable, but what I thought was just pride in taking care of how she looked as far as stylish clothes and cleanliness, held insecurity on my part. I didn't want people to think I was anything less than an exceptional mom. Many of us hope that if we keep our little ones well-groomed on the outside, that when people see our kids in town, they'll think, *what a cute kid*, or *that looks like a mom who has it together.* I was open to talking to other mothers about it, and many of them acknowledged that they too wanted people to think they were a good mom. There isn't anything wrong with striving to be the best possible parent. I felt secure about who I was as a mom in my head, because it was something I'd prepared for all of my life, and I had excellent role models. I knew with academic certainty that I was a loving mother, but I began to doubt this truth in a small corner of my mind after giving my baby over to abortion. It took nearly twenty years to realize that this accusatory voice was not from God, and it wasn't even from me. It was from a spiritual enemy who sought to disable me in any way that he could.

When dealing with one medical diagnosis after another, I kept asking each new doctor, "What's the root cause of this?" While doctors agreed that stress exacerbates many health conditions, no one ever asked if I was a perfectionist. As it is with secrets, it took an incredible amount of energy to hold back the floodgates of honesty. It was exhausting to pretend. Secrets held me in the grip of sharp teeth. I felt sure that if I moved toward escape, my wounds would widen. If I just stayed still and played dead, I thought the predator would grow bored and drop me from his mouth. But I sensed that if I played dead much longer my soul would smother and extinguish my pilot light. By staying silent about my past, I allowed depression and loneliness to grow stronger and louder. Sometimes the burdens we carry on the inside bubble up and out through our pores, and ultimately there is no buffer strong enough to insulate our body from the inward assaults of grief, depression, performance anxiety, and the exhausting flip-flopping of double-mindedness.

CHAPTER 26:

DOUBLE-MINDEDNESS

(2019)

One blustery fall day in October 2019, after a long and enjoyable inter-view to explore the possibility of volunteering at a local pregnancy resource center, I drove to my next errand acutely aware of traces of shame. There was a point during the interview when I saw an opportunity to share that I was an abortion survivor, but I stayed silent. The staff I met with were friendly, inspiring, and compassionate women of faith, and I passionately endorse the work they do to help pregnant women connect to vitally needed resources. It was important to me that they not think my desire to volunteer was in any way a form of penitence. I'd held off volunteering at a similar pregnancy resource center ten years prior because I knew I was not yet liv-ing in a place of emotional freedom. As my relationship deepened with my friends at the pregnancy resource center, I became aware of the balancing act I was caught in, walking along the top of a narrow picket fence, wobbling in dishonesty and double-mindedness.

When I arrived at my next stop, the local craft store, I found myself in the fabric aisle gathering up every roll of red grosgrain ribbon with white stitching I could find for a project. On my way to pay the cashier, I checked the description printed on the roll to see if the ribbon was "double-faced." I knew that it wasn't just my early upbringing that seared the concept of being double-faced or double-minded into my heart. What was building in me was conviction, conviction that I needed to be honest, and to let the back side of my imperfect ribbon, my imperfect story, show. While double-faced ribbon is prettier and more expensive, the word "two-faced" in the world of humanity conveys something quite different—a person who has two sides that don't match. This can be witnessed every day when someone is friendly and polite in public but speaks disparagingly of someone in private. A person may be publicly registered as a member of one political party yet privately vote for candidates of the opposing party. There is nothing wrong with the latter, but it's an example of how our outward indicators may sometimes conflict with our actions. In this context, I am not speaking about maliciousness, but rather mismatch. A person can nod in agreement in a social setting that pornography is bad yet indulge in this behavior in secret. I raised my child with a belief that sex outside of marriage had real consequences and was not part of God's design, in spite of knowing that I did not maintain my sexual purity before marriage. Mismatch.

In examining myself under the microscope, I noted that I typically chose to go peacefully along with the opinions of the group around me even when I disagreed. There were times when it was just easier to be polite. When I did this, I thought it was nothing more than the result of good home training and a form of social grace. But I had started to examine my motives, and I began to question if never disagreeing with others, simply to avoid conflict, was always the right thing. It was time to tell the truth, the whole truth, regardless of how many feathers it might ruffle.

My tendency to seek peace at any price was reinforced through my career in Human Resources, a role that highly valued diplomacy and peaceful conflict resolution. Once I became aware of my tendency to have a mismatch between what I said and how I felt, I realized I was doing it habitually. I doubted I was alone in the tendency to sway to the opinions of others out of fear of disapproval. I was restrained and professional in public settings, but at home I became unbridled by hyperbole and humor, arms flailing with a fiery temper. My love and investment in friends and family was real, but so was my abhorrence of conflict. Did my willingness to say things I didn't believe just to agree go much deeper than the fact that I had a first edition copy of Emily Post?

While my expression of opinions and emotions could see-saw between opposite realities, this also seemed true with my physical body. More than a half-dozen physical therapists involved in my care since 2000 described one of my primary musculoskeletal issues as what's called "hypermobility." Hypermobile joints tend to pair with lax ligaments and chronic tendonitis, contributing to loose joints that repeatedly reinjure. Unstable joints and ligament laxicity are often partnered with extreme tightness in the body's attempt to protect the joints.[14] Hence, someone can be both too loose and too tight at the same time. It seemed that even my body flip-flopped between two states of double-mindedness. Through years of medical appointments and physical therapy to manage chronic pain and muscle spasms, I learned about the many physiological explanations for these findings. Hypotheses ranged from early and long-term use of antibiotics, some of which can lead to tendon damage, to genetic predisposition to connective tissue disease. Other studies explained how elevated prolactin levels can contribute to lax ligaments, as the body mistakenly prepares for pregnancy that never comes.[15]

I've experienced countless massage therapy sessions in my life, but I have only experienced a strong emotional release during massage one time, though I did not share what I felt with the practitioner. One massage therapist I saw in 2002 remarked about a lack of responsiveness of my muscles and tissues to massage, and she was sure I had extreme tension and emotional blockage in my hip and pelvic area. I felt awkward and vulnerable staring at her commercial-grade carpet through the small window in the circular face mask of her massage table. I knew there was some truth to her statement, but I had no intention of sharing anything about the secrets of my past with her.

Years of counseling to care for my mind and heart taught me that the onset of my connective tissue disease and other symptoms occurred after the trauma of abortion. I was never able to touch my toes or get halfway toward the goal of doing the splits, indicating that this condition or precursors to it might have been present in my body as a child or written into my genetic code from birth. Certain disease states must first be present in our DNA for that condition to later be turned on or expressed. Internal or external stressors such as stress, inflammation, exposure to toxins or chemicals, other comorbid conditions, the absence of preventive health care or lack of emotional support may sometimes activate the expression of what is written in our genetic code. To oversimplify my example, in identical twins who both test positive for the presence of the BRCA gene for breast cancer, it is not always the case that both identical siblings will go on to get breast cancer.[16] Many factors can impact the expression of the breast cancer gene. Most of my life, I looked to anatomy and physiology to explain the medical diagnoses I faced in my life. However, I am learning that my body also carried tremendous unresolved emotional pain for two decades, and that the medical trauma of my abortion experience greatly impacted my physical health.

It has taken many years of growing in my faith through prayer and study of God's Word to begin to put my body, mind, heart, and soul back together in an effort to arrive at integration and, ultimately, acceptance. The Bible supplemented my learning to illustrate the hypocrisy of double-mindedness in many verses such as (Revelation 3:15-16) where lukewarm believers are scolded for being "neither cold nor hot" and warned that they might be "spit out" of God's mouth. My body was tired, and God was perhaps tiring of my tepid commitment. (Psalm 12:2) describes something I think we have all likely done at least once, "Everyone lies to their neighbor; they flatter with their lips but harbor deception in their hearts." I can almost hear Elijah of the Bible challenging me in (1 Kings 18:21) when he says, "How long will you waver between two opinions?"

The inner war I waged between two faces, two personas, two truths was exhausting. The cognitive dissonance over dueling realities was painfully present even in the decision to get pregnant with our second child. I wanted to have a sibling for Lily, and I was a maternal person, but I wasn't ready to have a second baby. I didn't speak up clearly or with conviction, and instead I gave in to Ben's pressure in an effort to keep the peace. I waffled in double-mindedness for months until getting pregnant made the decision for me. Once I learned I was pregnant, I allowed myself to be happy, and my heart immediately fell in love with our baby.

It was freeing to learn about the concept of the "extroverted introvert" and the idea of there being an introversion-extroversion spectrum—another free pass to better understand why I was outgoing and friendly with complete strangers, but then retreated to my quiet home wanting nothing more than to be alone to recharge. The longer I knew my post-abortive self, the more I realized the tension of living between two realities in my physical body and in my thought life. The outward evidence of my mothering skills was visible in my daughter's healthy development, but in the darkest part of my heart I doubted if I was truly a good mother. One side of my double-faced ribbon reality showed a beautiful relationship with my living child, but on the back side of the ribbon, I was a mother who had denied my second child the chance to be a miracle.

I knew where I stood on the issue of abortion in private, but I lacked the courage to hold this position in public. While I was proud of a modest number of accomplishments in my life, I was ashamed of my hesitancy to speak out on the topic of abortion. What held me back from going public as a deeply changed and now pro-life woman? I knew the answer well, as it often held me in its shackles—the fear of the loss of approval. I still feared that open admission of my abortion would cut my list of friends in half or that friends would disappear altogether. It also hurt to think that by stepping over the line to support the pro-life movement, I could offend or alienate other people I loved. As a Christian, I accepted that I had a real enemy who knew all the details about my high need for approval and my sincere desire to never hurt anyone's feelings. This was my Achilles' heel. In my life, I had been both fierce and fearful. I knew I had done something wrong, and I didn't want anyone to know. The microscope and microphone of social media made my predicament tangible and obvious.

Consider David, one of the Bible's beloved heroes, who was both a king and a scoundrel, an unexpected underdog chosen by divine appointment, yet strong enough to defeat Goliath through a powerful faith and trust that God would make him victorious. He was a lover caught in an affair that resulted in an illegitimate child—a situation that led him to commit murder—yet he was also a passionate and sincere lover of God. He knew his affair with Bathsheba was wrong, and he lamented his sin of sending her husband Uriah to the front lines of the battlefield to die. He knew the pain of grief when their firstborn son died as an infant. Yet in spite of his raw humanity and his sinful nature, he relentlessly pursued God to return to a right relationship with Him. His words remain as powerful today as they were then.

"Have mercy on me, O God, according to your unfailing love; according to your great compassion blot out my transgressions." (Psalm 51:1)

"Teach me your way, Lord, that I may rely on your faithfulness; give me an undivided heart, that I may fear your name." (Psalm 86:11)

Through my relationship with God and the person of Jesus Christ, I was being healed and released into greater freedom of an undivided heart like David.

CHAPTER 27:

ORPHANED BOUQUET

(2019)

"Do you want to pick a new one from this box?"

I walked toward the floral counter without seeing the employee right in front of me.

Had she been talking to me? My brain fog began to clear, and I could see that she was sliding a box of fresh bouquets in my direction across the stainless-steel countertop.

"Oh, I'm sorry. I didn't hear you."

She repeated the question that had been intended for me. "Do you want to pick a new one from this box? The other bouquets are starting to fade a bit."

"Oh, thank you. Sure. How nice." All I really wanted to say was, *I'm happy with the bouquet I have in my hand,* but if there was any risk of slighting someone, even a complete stranger, I couldn't speak freely about what I wanted. I selected a beautiful mini bouquet from her fresh shipment, but it had pink roses and not the cranberry red ones I had already chosen that looked much more appropriate for autumn. I thanked her two more times before walking to the check stand across the aisle to pay, thinking to myself, *He was a boy. How did I end up with pink roses?*

The awkward bouquet experience continued when I got to the park for my annual visit to the pond. Children were screaming with energy and glee all around the play structure, and the only people my age were walking in pairs or at least walking a dog. No one seemed to take notice because I looked like a mom or a grandma at the park who was there for carpool pickup, but I felt odd because I was carrying a small clutch of flowers. I held the pink bouquet in the same hand with my cell phone and keys to minimize it.

Nothing to see here, I admonished my nearby park cohorts.

I should have thought to bring earbuds or something to help me better fit in as a park walker, but the mild limp from my hip and ankle kept me at a shuffle. I stopped along the way to take photos of the kaleidoscope colors that made each tree look like a watercolor painting. Perhaps this was the prettiest autumn of all, I thought, even though I'd said the same thing to myself every year for nineteen years walking on this path. If I could just make it to the gazebo by the pond, then the flowers would be out of sight to other people. I felt self-conscious on so many levels, and because the sun was out in Seattle, the park was full of families walking behind school-aged children on bikes. New moms running with jogging strollers and dog walking middle-aged men in zipped-up fleece jackets kept passing me along the trail. I only needed a minute to take photos of the flowers in a few of the park's most scenic spots. My plan was to pull off rose petals and toss them into the pond, something I had never done before, but access to the edge of the water proved slippery from the wet and decomposing leaves breaking down into a cornucopia of mulch. I took a picture of the bouquet of pink flowers posed on a rustic bench, lying on a moss-covered rock, propped up on the bench inside the gazebo, and nestled on top of the leaves at the pond's edge. Throwing them into the pond wasn't going to work, and I felt awkward again. In the shelter of the gazebo, I took my place on the bench thinking

I should make myself sit quietly and pray. I was immediately interrupted by a gaggle of teenage girls coming up the path right behind me.

Please turn around and walk away, girls. I wished they could hear my silent thoughts, but they didn't get the hint, and I was forced to leave prematurely.

I left the orphaned bouquet at the water's edge, and I decided to be at peace with where it rested. Walking through the fall foliage around me, I asked God if there was anything, I was supposed to better understand this year. Each annual visit to the pond usually gifted me with something in this journey of grief, whether small or profound, but I wasn't feeling much of anything beyond a quiet respect for the day. I couldn't think of anything to say other than to whisper in my mind, *I'm here again, little one. I still come every year, and I love you.*

My throat felt tight as I thought, *If God can forgive me, and you can forgive me, I think it's time I finally forgive myself.*

On that day in the nineteenth year of my grief, after years of reading and studying scripture I finally made the head connection that God *could* forgive me, that He *would* forgive me, and that He *had* forgiven me. Forgiveness for my abortion was granted the moment I confessed my first regret to the Lord, and my repentance didn't need to be rehearsed, redone, or ritualized. I had been the only remaining obstacle between my heart and God's forgiveness. I didn't need to hang myself up on a cross of my own making. I only needed to sit at the foot of the cross of a loving Savior who would stand in the gap for me. All I had to do was to take one step toward Jesus, and He was close enough to catch me as I collapsed from the exhaustion of carrying the heaviness of unforgiveness to which I'd sentenced myself all these years. Jesus was waiting to wrap me up in His unconditional love, and He wanted to heal me of my heartbreak.

When I finally let go of my lingering inhibitions that day, I felt a weight begin to lift off my burning shoulders. As I relaxed into His strong arms, my chest became lighter, and I breathed in deeply, as if I had surfaced from holding my breath under water for far too long. At first out of breath, I began to go limp, crying tears of relief that felt cleansing as they washed old wounds with their healing salts. Allowing myself to be held in the arms of Jesus felt safe, and my scarred heart began to beat again in time with the start of a brand-new day.

CHAPTER 28:

NO HAPPY ENDINGS

(2020)

It is hard to believe that the medical community can put the word therapeutic in the same sentence with the word abortion. There is nothing therapeutic about the procedure, the experience, the recovery, or the aftermath for the mother, the father, or anyone involved.

I recognize that there are women for whom an abortion may have led to freedom, to relief, to a new chapter, or somehow to peace. Regardless of a person's individual feelings on this painful medical reality, therapeutic medical abortion never leads to a happy ending. A happy ending for parents of a wanted pregnancy is to come home from the hospital in nine months with a baby. I allege that the majority of babies given a poor prognosis, often not diagnosed until the 16 week of pregnancy or later, are wanted. It is not my place to say which pregnancies are wanted or unwanted in the hearts of mothers. Perhaps because only 6.9% of abortions are performed between 14-20 weeks of gestation, and abortions beyond the 21 week only make up 1.3% of these annual statistics, there seems a significant lack of honest stories published about this segment of the population.[17]

I recognize that every day there are countless women who have abortions for many reasons. Unless I have walked in the shoes of a woman, I imagine her decision is as unique as the fingerprint on the underside of her

thumb. I don't believe it's my job to judge her. I allege that her healing journey is hers alone. Women living with post-abortion trauma have enough to
carry, and when society throws harsh words of judgment, labeling them as
"sinners," it does the opposite of fostering healing. Countless stories in the
Bible beautifully illustrate Jesus inviting sinners into one-on-one moments,
and He approaches them with love and compassion. Jesus doesn't avoid the
sin. He's direct, and He tells the characters in the Bible to "go and sin no
more." (John 8:11 [NKJV]) But He doesn't stone them to death. He doesn't
reject them. He never shames them. In Mark 5, we meet a woman who has
suffered for twelve years in poor health from chronic menstrual bleeding. She
had seen many doctors and spent all the money she had trying to get better,
but she got worse. "When she heard about Jesus, she came up behind him in
the crowd and touched his cloak." (Mark 5:27) In spite of being surrounded
on all sides by crowds of people, Jesus felt power go out of Him, and He
asked, "Who touched my clothes?" (Mark 5:30) When the woman came
forward with fear and fell at His feet, Jesus spoke kindly to her, "Daughter,
your faith has healed you. Go in peace and be freed from your suffering."
(Mark 5:34) Condemnation and the use of shame to convince others of our
belief in the sanctity of life can create distance between people and drive
the abortion wounded into deeper silence and shame.

Jesus not only led with love and forgiveness, but He often used some
of the best scratch and dent models in the Bible to accomplish pivotal things
for the Kingdom of God—people like Moses, Joseph, Gideon, Paul, and
so many others. When I began to understand that God uses the weak, the
imperfect, and the wounded, my life felt less like something for the recycle bin
and more like something worthy of being cleaned, polished, and upcycled.

My story of overcoming abortion trauma bears no comparison to
the heroes of the Bible. Our loss was a story of two flawed people, in an
imperfect marriage, who were faced with a devastating prenatal diagnosis
and were immediately encircled by a united front of leading-edge medical
professionals who advised us of only one option. Who were we to argue
with an obstetrician, a radiologist, and a genetic counselor who told us

without hesitation to terminate our pregnancy? My husband was a devotee to science, worked in the medical industry, and was an impassioned atheist. I was a tenuous and seeking Christian just learning about the Bible and the person of Jesus Christ, but I had not yet taken the next step in praying to accept Jesus into my heart, nor had I chosen to publicly acknowledge my faith through baptism. When we received the most devastating news of our lives, Ben and I were living in a secular world and would have never thought to seek God in prayer for direction in our decision. I was also primed with an intense respect for Western medicine, and I believed everything a doctor told me. Unfortunately, that was our universe, our perspective, and our bias at the time.

No matter the backdrop of the lives of mothers like myself—whether it be financial stress, a marriage in shreds, or an unplanned pregnancy—I think that many mothers who continue into the second trimester begin to reconcile their pregnancies. And if a poor fetal diagnosis arises later in gestation, most of these mothers have already fallen in love with the tiny flutters in their bellies. As a Christian, I believe that the gift of life comes to a mother because she is chosen for the task. Even a woman who may feel like a nobody, once an expectant mother, becomes someone special in a new way—she becomes someone's mother.

If a woman has an abortion, it is done and is in the past. Someone who has endured an abortion has surrendered a child and survived it. Abortion is a controversial word and a controversial topic for many reasons, the hardest of which to speak is that it puts the decision to end a life into the hands of humans and takes it out of the hands of God. Most mothers instinctively long to protect their baby's life, but the darkest truth at the center of abortion is the decision to say yes to ending a life. After an abortion, a woman can slip out of a hospital gown and take some comfort in the familiarity of her street clothes, returning to the sights and sounds of a seemingly normal life, but more than a baby is taken from her that day. If a woman chooses to go through with the procedure, she's going to need someone to love her rather than judge her, someone to listen to her as she walks through the grief process. Anti-inflammatories and time can heal a woman's reproductive system, but for some there is no length of time that proves an ample balm for the damage to the soul.

We complicate issues of human suffering when we look through lenses that are biased by our political beliefs, our gender, our religious positions and our opinions. It's inherently human for us to have different perspectives, but when someone is suffering, I believe we should act. The lenses I look through as a Christian woman give me specific laws and commands from God that I strive to follow, but these laws don't restrict my ability to reach out with compassion. Jesus forgave, and He helped people stand themselves up and start a new chapter—a beautiful example of compassion in action. One day in heaven, I look forward to understanding the giant quilt God is making with the individual stories of our humanity. Until then, I find peace in wondering if part of the reason my son came was to reconcile me with the Son.

Where I stand on the issue of abortion today is profoundly different from where I stood twenty years ago, but I can't go back in time and choose differently. My heart has been changed to believe that pro-choice leaves expectant mothers with few choices. I think back on my twenty-nine-year-old self, afraid and alone in the recovery room, and I want to tell her "it's going to be okay." I wish I could have told her that on the heels of the greatest loss in her life, she had a Savior waiting to hear her cries—cries just as broken and earnest as those of King David. A Savior waits for us all, waiting to lift survivors up with a warm and steady hand, with eyes of empathy, and a heart of forgiveness. Little did I know that my Savior was patiently waiting for me on a mountaintop two thousand miles away.

CHAPTER 29:

ROYALTY

(2020)

2020 was a momentous year in America and around the world, as mankind faced the dark foe of a global pandemic. Natural disasters, war, and civil unrest didn't stop to turn down the steam on the pressure cooker of creation. It was a significant year in my personal life as well, as I finished writing the manuscript for my book, and I worked hard to sweep out the remaining cobwebs of shame and regret from my mind and heart. One of the positive consequences of the pandemic in my life was that it created pockets of time for consistent Bible study, greater introspection, and prayer. After reading Karen Ellison's book and learning more about her ministry called Deeper Still, I committed to attend an abortion healing retreat in Knoxville, Tennessee. I was scheduled to go in July, but the quarantine restrictions in the U.S. caused me to reschedule my trip to October, a beautiful time of year to visit the Great Smoky Mountains. Feeling that I was in a solid place with my manuscript, I was confident that the retreat would be a special time to celebrate a finished work with the Lord.

As I made my way up the switchbacks of the famous US-129 in an upgraded sportscar rental—a highway also known as the Tail of the Dragon—I felt excited and anxious for the retreat weekend to start. A veteran of the summer camps of my youth, I was prepared to share meals with strangers in a dining hall and to sing and worship with other believers, as I was accustomed to doing at church. I pulled off the road frequently to take pictures of the green pastures and rolling hills of Tennessee covered with fall foliage of every conceivable shade of amber and orange and yellow. The sky felt big and open, punctuated by low-hanging cumulous clouds that cast a clear topcoat on the autumn colors. I wanted to remember the beauty of this drive and the twenty-year journey that had brought me to this place, to the openness and vulnerability I knew would be required of me at the top of this unfamiliar mountain halfway across the country.

I had talked to God about the retreat for weeks, regularly handing Him my excitement, my concerns, and my anxieties. Making the trip alone without my husband to help me with the luggage and travel details would be a feat, as I managed the ongoing challenges of insomnia and chronic pain and migraine. I was determined to prove to him, to my family, and to myself that I could handle this solo adventure. It was a long two weeks of preparation, packing and re-packing to get myself to this moment, driving through the beautiful gated entrance of the retreat center. I gasped out loud in my car at the sight of the property, its beauty and a welcoming ease of the trees and the house. Arriving about thirty minutes early, I found a place to park, and cracked the car window open to listen in case anyone was to call out to redirect my parking efforts or to welcome me early. I gathered my front seat belongings and reorganized my purse, tugging at the rear-view mirror to inspect for out-of-place strands of hair or any crumbs on my face from the peanut butter crackers that had been my mobile lunch. Taking a deep breath, I sat in the warmth of the car ready to change gears in my mind. I began to notice a choir of cicadas as their melody rose up from the trees, and I turned in my seat to look at the house, struck by the most majestic view I had ever seen. The house had a wraparound porch, and from where I parked, I could see that it faced the Smokies without obstruction—a panoramic view of the mountains, shrouded in ethereal clouds and a sea of trees in the peak of their October color. I rolled down the window to take in the full splendor of the scene.

"Wow!" I whispered audibly.

"Thank you, God for getting me here."

I sat quietly for a few minutes, not wanting to be the first guest to arrive. I stared at the mountains in reverent silence. God spoke to my spirit two years before when He asked me to write my story, and here surrounded by the song of the cicadas, as clearly as if He was sitting right beside me, I heard one word:

Royalty.

I'd had no idea how long it would take to write a book. When I first sat down to scribble the first chapter, I was nearly housebound and disabled by crippling migraines and other health challenges. I set small and attainable bite-sized goals along the way, and most days the pain of sitting at my laptop was excruciating if I worked beyond twenty minutes. Once I could see the manuscript taking shape around a scaffold of post-it notes and poster paper on the walls of my office, I gained momentum, but the process of editing and rewriting kept unraveling into a longer and longer chain of tasks and details. I had a general idea of my ultimate deadline, but only God knew that I would complete my final round of edits on the twentieth anniversary of Nathanael's birthday. Only God knew that I would accept an invitation to attend an abortion healing retreat clear across the country during a global pandemic, and that through a mountaintop experience, He would meet me there with a majestic welcome befitting a princess. This is the God we serve—the God of the Bible, the God of Moses and Jacob and David. He is the God who met Joseph at the bottom of a well, Jonah in the belly of a fish, and Paul in the dark depths of a prison. He is the God of forgiveness, mercy, and redemption who loves us no matter our station or our circumstance. If we are willing to cry out to Him, He will meet us, He will take our hand, and He will lift us up out of the pit and exchange our tattered rags for the adornment of royalty.

CHAPTER 30:

LOST

The online support groups to which I belonged in the first year after the abortion described parents in our situation as those who made "the compassionate choice." I spent years feeling confident that we had spared our son pain and premature death. We were told that if he survived, he would have faced many post-natal surgeries and unimaginable pain. One neonatologist asked us to consider the impact our son's medical outcome might have on our living child, who was two years old at the time. By making the decision to end our pregnancy, I was painted in an almost heroic way, transferring the suffering from our innocent baby onto my own body. I took comfort from one online community that essentially said I paid the price to spare our child terrible suffering later. It was true that I did pay a price. My body had kept score physically, mentally, emotionally, and spiritually. I do not, however, believe that the manner in which our son's life ended spared him suffering. In fact, I think that the procedure that rendered him lifeless before his time likely caused him pain. I also believe that had he been given the chance to further develop, and if he'd been born alive—even if he had died within hours or days—that my merciful God would have looked after him with a legion of angels. I have reconciled my double-minded heart that can simultaneously respect and love people who view medically advised abortion as compassionate while committing to a pro-life position for myself. I give others room to formulate and take comfort in their own beliefs, their own coping strategies, and their own faith. I respect and care for the dear people who were there for me in the early years of my grief who offered validation that I needed to hear. Believing that terminating the pregnancy of our wanted son was the right thing to do was something I clung to like a life raft slowly losing air. At the time, we felt it was the best decision we could make, but justifying it for nearly two decades was a lie that left me adrift and lost.

Healing from abortion did not require the completion of a complex, unattainable rubric. Through faith in Jesus, the Holy Spirit came to take up residence in my heart, and His power gave me strength—strength to reach out in vulnerability to speak the truth of what I had done. Once my silence was broken, deeper connection with others became possible, and as I felt less alone, the veil of shame began to lift, allowing forgiveness to reveal its simplicity first to my mind and ultimately to my heart.

The pain of losing a child, born or unborn, is real and carries with it the physical impact of grief, which can be detected through our vital signs of blood pressure, heart rate, and responsiveness to people and external stimuli. The other components of loss, such as emotional devastation, may arrive immediately or be delayed, and for some can last a lifetime. Loss through no fault of our own is easier to rationalize. If I lose my way during GPS navigation, lose a wallet, or even lose a grandparent, I react on a continuum ranging from momentary frustration to a season of grief commensurate with the depth of my relationship to the loved one. If I lose my keys, aside from some initial panic, it's not the end of the world. If someone loses a child, it's quite a different thing.

Few people discount how a person is forever changed by the loss of a child. This kind of grief is universal in every culture around the world. It's no surprise that the loss of a child is one of the greatest known life stressors.[18] People don't always know what to say to a grieving parent, but most are moved to compassion in their hearts. An employee could pick up the workload of a grieving coworker or sign up for a meal train in a coordinated effort to keep the family well stocked with food. Most people will send a card, post a social media message of concern, or put a gentle hand on the heavy shoulder of a suffering parent to offer their condolences.

I often take issue with the word "lost." While it makes sense to say we have lost our cell phone or lost a receipt, to say we have lost a person hits me wrong. When something is lost, by definition, it is misplaced. If someone dies at the age of ninety-one and has lived a long and rich life, are they misplaced? I think, rather, they are in a very real place. People who die are not in a state of misplacement; they're in a destination. The same is true with a "lost" child who has passed away. Many with a spiritual belief system assert that lost loved ones are in a utopian place like heaven, and if we accept this truth, it is easier for our rational minds to imagine where they have gone. For many, the idea of heaven brings peace and accelerates the healing process during grief. While grief is an ongoing cycle with different phases, it often raises its head again and again. Over the years, in a deeply personal way for each individual, the bereaved who have adequate support and coping mechanisms hope to ultimately arrive at a place of closure. Closure does not mean we are void of memories of a deceased loved one, or that there are no longer triggers that bring the lost to mind. However, closure, if attainable, can be a place of less anxiety and greater peace, like standing on firm ground after surviving long seasons of shifting sand.

What are we to do with the unborn? Can a baby be lost who was never born? How do we lose an infant who was never seen or held? How do we comfort parents who come home from the hospital with empty arms? There was a point in my grief when the expression "lost a baby" made me angry. I didn't lose my baby. It was more accurate to say that my baby was taken—torn from me in a way that was too difficult to comprehend for many years.

I didn't misplace my baby. His life was extinguished by a medical professional with my knowledge and with my permission. After years of post-abortive trauma, I began to tire of lying when someone asked if I had other children and feeling like the only appropriate reply was to say "no." Answering with a lie accomplished something safe in the experience of the hearer by giving them a simple and finite answer. Yet what the lies accomplished in my soul each time I told them was to remind me that what I had done was too horrific to admit, too shameful to share, too honest to be heard.

CHAPTER 31:

FOUND

Abortion is a word frequently heard on the news, but it is rarely spoken out loud in the personal lives of those who have survived it. It is not only an uncomfortable word, it's an uncomfortable choice. It's a choice that once it is in the past should never be met with judgment or shame. Women and expecting parents who have survived the abortion experience should be approached with open minds, open hearts, and open arms ready to receive them with compassion. A woman who has experienced abortion may suffer from many emotional, behavioral, and spiritual wounds, and I believe that if we are brave enough to listen to the stories of mothers of abortion, we will find recurring themes of life-altering and soul-damaging trauma. Each mother and each story is unique, but I think common to every abortion is a woman who, without adequate support, is left in a state of grief that is compounded by silence, secrecy, and shame. Women heal differently and at different rates based on the complex details of their lives, their support structures, and their personal value systems. I am certain there are many women who can reach a significant state of healing much earlier in the grief process than I did.

For me, the trauma of the abortion of a wanted and loved child, drawn out by negligent medical care left indelible marks on my body, mind, and soul. These marks caused collateral damage that manifested itself in my physical body in the form of a hypervigilant physical state that led to chronic insomnia, inflammation, pain, migraine, autoimmune disease, connective tissue disease, and ultimately, cancer. My behavioral health was deeply impacted by shame which increased generalized anxiety. Over time, attempts to manage painful medical conditions, exhaustion and anxiety, PTSD, and situational medical depression intensified maladaptive behaviors such as double-mindedness and perfectionism to cover my wounds and mask the ugliness I felt. It took twenty years to understand these connections and to learn healthier ways of taking care of my body and my spirit.

I don't have a magic pill to cure the chronic medical conditions that I live with, but I am well on the way to acceptance and peace with the body I have and the story it tells. The latter part of my twenty-year grief journey led me to new understanding of how trauma impacted my spiritual growth and how shame served as a roadblock to the freedom found in God's grace. Much like the Israelites, I wandered in the desert for decades, unaware that I was punishing myself in ways that were cruel, unforgiving, and incompatible with the person of Jesus Christ. While I appeared to have my life together on the outside, I was utterly lost.

There is no reason to live like you're lost when you can be found. There is also no reason to live a life of secrecy, shame, and isolation following an abortion, because we serve a God who has compassion beyond our imagination, who not only can, but *has* forgiven our sins—all of our sins. We only need to bring God a repentant heart. Abortion is not an unforgiveable sin. Be reminded of the thief on the cross next to Jesus who was forgiven in the last moments of his life and went to be with Him in paradise. (Luke 23:42-43)

In the year 2000, I made the best decision I could with the information I had at the time. I no longer waver on the fact that I also made the biggest mistake of my life. I stand humbled by a God who can take my greatest regrets and turn them into something more beautiful than I could imagine. Never again will I say that my baby was lost, for it was I who was lost. It was in the wandering where grief led me to the Lord who brought me out of shame and into connection, forgiveness, acceptance, and ultimately to freedom. As great a tragedy as it was, my son's death paved the way to me being found. My Nathanael was formed by a Creator who breathed life and beauty into him—a child I will one day see. I had the honor of being chosen to be his mother, if only for a short time, out of the unfathomable mercy of a God who was determined to find a way to finally reach me.

Redemption is the act of gaining something in exchange for payment. My son was given in an exchange that nearly killed me, but ultimately saved my life. I am only one mother of millions, a grain of sand and seemingly insignificant. Yet we serve a God who considers no one insignificant, and He offers the greatest exchange of the life of His one and only Son, Jesus, to save us for all eternity if we believe. "If you declare with your mouth, 'Jesus is Lord,' and believe in your heart that God raised him from the dead, you will be saved." (Romans 10:9) Our part is simple: accept the unmerited grace of Jesus, and He will set you free. "So if the Son sets you free, you will be free indeed." (John 8:36)

The shackles of shame I wore around my heart were of my own making. They were never put there by God. In some ways, I chose to take on the mantle meant only for God by passing judgment on myself with no possibility of pardon or parole. I took authority over determining which sins in my life were forgivable and which were unforgiveable. I set my own rules that were not based on the truth of the Bible. God's Word is embroidered throughout every page with love and grace and forgiveness. As I grew in my relationship with Christ and further studied scripture, I saw countless examples of Bible characters who were fallible, selfish, corrupt, and evil, yet time after time God gave them chances to learn from their mistakes and to start anew. There was no one standing in the way of the free gift of forgiveness that God was offering except me.

I called myself a Christian, I believed in Jesus Christ, and I had invited Him into my life. In fact, He stood in the gap, interceding for me with an outstretched arm that never grew tired as He waited and waited year after year for me to accept His unconditional love. I watched friend after friend find healing and forgiveness and peace, but I deemed myself unworthy of receiving that same gift. I was the problem. I was the obstacle in the way of my own freedom. Twenty years after my abortion, I cried out to Him again, desperate for closure in my healing. He unlocked my self-imposed chains, and I was free. There was no required ritual, no formal ceremony, just the simple act of talking to God as a friend, with a broken and repentant heart, and He was there. He had always been there. I stopped punishing myself with endless penitence. I stopped wandering in the desert and looked up. He was there.

This is my story—a story of a baby conceived within a marriage. A baby who would have made a two-year-old little girl a big sister. A baby onto whom hopes of saving a broken marriage were mistakenly pinned. A baby for whom a list of names was expectantly scribbled. A baby nourished by prenatal vitamins, preventive medical care, and good nutrition. A baby who was sung to, wanted, dreamed of, and loved. My situation may not fit society's poster story of a mother who has had an abortion, but I know I do not suffer post-abortion trauma alone. I don't find it my place to lobby, legislate, or lecture people into being pro-life over pro-choice. I know which side God is on, and I live out the layers of pain that came along with exercising the free will God gave us that day, but I will forever regret our decision. It is my hope that women who have experienced abortion can find freedom in reading a real and raw story that helps them to feel less alone, less ashamed, and closer to healing.

I will never be found standing outside of Planned Parenthood. I don't plan to stand along a highway holding up poster board signs of aborted fetuses, torn apart and mangled. I appreciate the hearts of those who bring passion to their cause, but without meaningful dialogue, the images on these signs can further wound post-abortive parents. I don't find it necessary to solely use Bible verses to weave together an argument against abortion. The Word of God speaks for itself. I speak for me. I am thankful every day that God helped me come to resolution and healing from my abortion. When I finally let God navigate, He led me out of my own self-made obstacle course. God stands ready and waiting to offer compassion, forgiveness, and healing. Jesus does not condemn people even in the act of sinning, but He is honest. Jesus does not use shame to motivate people to turn away from things that are harming them. He offers compassion and His unmerited grace, and Jesus still offers His stripes upon a cross so that we may be forgiven, washed clean, as white as snow.

I commit to spending the rest of my life learning about and supporting the compassionate people who are working hard to foster abortion healing ministries. I stand in full support of pregnancy resource centers that offer tangible physical resources, loving support, and hope to pregnant women. I will not be found screaming through a megaphone for people to repent. I will, however, make myself available to talk to anyone on the difficult topic of abortion, with my ears and heart open to listen. My place may not be at the forefront of a movement, but I can be found at the shoulders of women who have survived abortion and wish they could go back. And every year on the eleventh of November, I can be found amidst the fall leaves under a Pacific Northwest sky at a gazebo that sits by a pond.

Natty's Pond

SOMATOFORM DISORDER

I cannot close this book without giving attention to the relationship between abortion trauma and its contribution to changes in the brain and body of survivors. Digging into the research necessary to write a book led me to read stories of other post-abortive women plagued with health issues that sounded eerily familiar to my own. When my health began to decline following my abortion, I blamed the litany of PTSD symptoms and my diagnoses of fibromyalgia, autoimmune disease, and even cancer on my own lack of physical and mental fortitude. I pinned these anxieties and cognitive changes to my self-worth, believing that I'd not simply been diagnosed with one medical issue after another because of my DNA and bad luck, but because I wasn't strong enough to be victorious over my health. As I began to read about some commonalities found in the health histories of abortion survivors, I was struck and saddened to learn that I was not alone. Regardless of growing research on the relationship between trauma and health, I am not saying that abortion *causes* health issues, but rather that there are strong correlations. I encourage readers to conduct their own research and formulate a personal position.

There is a long line of psychologists who believe that the body can hold on to past experiences, which can be released through bodywork—therapies and techniques which involve touching or manipulating the body. There is substantial data in support of this theory, and it is common for people to experience emotional release during modalities such as massage therapy, that traditional psychotherapy cannot access.[19] Few debate that there is a mind-body interconnection, and there are entire scientific disciplines devoted to this study and practice, one of which is called somatic psychology.[20] It studies relationships between our bodies and our thoughts and actions. Some believe that memories of trauma can be stored in an organism's body.

For those who prefer to think about the human experience from an evolutionary perspective, there are adaptive reasons why remembering trauma vividly can benefit us so that we avoid the pain of having a similar experience again.[21] Post Traumatic Stress Disorder (PTSD), anxiety, and depression can also lead to an increased likelihood of developing fibromyalgia. Dr. Bruce Solitar, clinical associate professor of medicine in the division of rheumatology at NYU Langone Orthopedic Hospital for Joint Diseases shares, "The [current] consensus is that fibromyalgia is not a problem with the muscles, joints, or tendons, but rather a problem with the central nervous system."[22] For those interested in studying the relationship between the brain, mind, and how the body processes trauma through rewiring of the brain, I highly recommend the book *The Body Keeps the Score* by Bessel van der Kolk, M.D.

Some believe that all fibromyalgia patients have been through emotional trauma. Fibromyalgia tends to run in families, and other underlying diseases such as arthritis can increase the chances of developing fibromyalgia.[23] Emotional trauma or physical abuse changes the way our brain perceives pain and stress.[24] The widespread pain of fibromyalgia was long shrouded in mystery, subject to diagnostic subjectivity and social stigma.

Women are significantly more likely to develop fibromyalgia than men, which is believed to be related to differences in the way men and women perceive pain.[25] For no other reason than the fact that women are the ones who carry, labor, and give birth to babies, it seems logical that women might perceive pain differently from men.

Reading about PTSD in post-abortive women, I came across the topic of Post Abortion Stress Syndrome, (PASS), defined simply as the psychological effects of abortion. The symptoms of PASS align closely with PTSD, and include feelings of intense guilt, anxiety, feelings of depression and numbness, flashbacks, and even suicidal thoughts.[26] While there remains debate about using the classification of PASS, there are many subsets under the current *DSM (Diagnostic and Statistical Manual of Mental Disorders)* discussion of PTSD related to postpartum and post-abortive complications. There are also ICD (International Classification of Disease) diagnosis codes specifically used for office visits for the purposes of elective termination of pregnancy, many types of abortions, and related complications. These consultative visits and abortive procedures are frequently covered by insurance and must have associated diagnosis and procedure codes (Current Procedural Terminology-CPT) for the processing of claims payments to medical providers and other professionals. I believe that the existence of these many codes validates the reality of abortion complications both physical and psychological. In my career as a licensed insurance professional, I have never seen diagnosis codes generate payment from an insurance company without those codes undergoing a stringent vetting process. Insurance companies rarely pay for things that are mere conjecture, as some opponents of the diagnosis of PASS allege it to be.

People may forever debate the complex interaction between nature vs. nurture, genetics and exposure, and the relationship between the mind and the body, but it is my hope that post-abortive women suffering from medical conditions like fibromyalgia, PTSD, and other chronic health issues can find encouragement in the new and emerging body of research that offers education and hope.

IN RECOGNITION

OF PERINATAL HOSPICE

There is a tremendous organization and ministry called Isaiah's Promise that reaches out to parents facing a life-limiting prenatal diagnosis. These families are counseled and wrapped in love, compassion, support, and tangible gifts to help them see these heartbreaking pregnancies through to completion. Connections and friendships are made, and the organization supports the family through the delivery and grief process. While I wish I had known then about organizations like Isaiah's Promise that exist today, the best thing I can do is to honor their work by passing along the information. Isaiah's Promise and other groups are humbly serving as the very hands and feet of Jesus for countless grieving families.

Other resources and web links on the topic of perinatal hospice and neonatal palliative care are listed at the end of this book. There you will also find an extensive bibliography, as well as a list of books and websites on the topic of healing from abortion.

IN REVERENCE
TO CATHOLICISM

One of the more difficult aspects of writing this book was discerning how to remain simultaneously true to my story and true to the memories of my thirteen years of Catholic school. As an important point of clarification, I want to confirm that I grew up as a non-Catholic student, which contributed to a feeling of being on the outside looking in, yet I was fully immersed in the daily practices of the faith. I ask my readers for grace and understanding that I did not receive catechism classes, nor do I profess to be an expert on any theological tenets of Catholicism. The scenes presented in this book represent my individual memories which are fallible and are unique to my developmental age and stage at the time.

I want to express my respect for friends and colleagues of the Catholic faith and acknowledge that there is no judgment or agenda on my part meant to be a commentary about the genuineness of one faith over another. Whether my reader identifies as an atheist, a protestant, a Catholic, an evangelical, or participates in any other form of worship, all are valuable and lend meaning and order to our world.

I am deeply thankful for the quality of education and the foundational principles of Christian faith that I received as a student of Catholic education. My thirteen years of parochial school contributed positively to who I am today, and the stories related in this memoir, while formative, only represent a portion of my experience. Regardless of my collection of childhood experience from which I took away some negative messages, I still hold the religion of my youth in high regard, with the utmost respect, and with a lasting reverence that I feel today. May we continue to work together across all faiths and denominations to honor God and foster acts of love and charity to mankind.

ACKNOWLEDGEMENTS

I wrote my story based on journal entries and medical records, but all human memory is fallible. I had no intention to cause anyone harm, and to that aim the names of people and places have been changed.

While it was academically tenable to type over 68,000 words of text for this book because there was much to say, the physical and emotional pain of writing was daunting. The spiritual work of telling this story resulted in growth beyond my expectations and deep spiritual discoveries that were tenderly orchestrated by God. Each time I asked Jesus to join me on this journey, He reminded me that He was already in my heart and at my side. My greatest acknowledgement goes to Father God, the kindest gentleman of my life.

I could write a page for each person I wish to thank for their support. For my friend and mentor, Karen Foster—it will take a lifetime of continued friendship to invest in your heart the way you have invested in mine. For Charlene Wallace Moy—your steadfast friendship, hours of your time, and your acceptance of the real me gave me confidence. For Karen Yates—the joy of our adventures and your unconditional friendship lifts my spirits daily. For Tiffani, my friend of over thirty years—the peace of knowing you reside in my heart helped me find my voice. To the ladies of my Bible study group and the many women in my life who I call friends (and you know who you are), thank you for your compassion and unconditional support while I wrote this book. I also wish to thank Jeannette Heffley who helped me find the courage to speak publicly about my story at church for the very first time.

To the women who began as strangers but who responded to my phone calls and emails with love, compassion and encouragement, I thank you for taking a chance on my story. This list is not all-inclusive, but I wish to thank Nancy Mayer-Whittington, Peggy Hartshorn, Betty McDowell, Deaconess Georgette Forney, Sheila Harper, Carol Everett, Kathy Collard Miller, Serena Dyksen, and Jeannie Pittam.

For Greg Hasek, who lent hours of his time from across the country to hear me and to lend his breadth of insight into the depths of the trauma of abortion for both men and women, I am forever thankful for your generosity.

For Karen A. Ellison, there are not enough words to thank you for the healing found in your book and your anointed ministry of Deeper Still. Your words both written and spoken to me in empathy and solidarity have blessed my life in ways that are still blooming.

Thank you, Pat Layton for your beautiful and inspired book and ministry materials, and for how you opened the door for me to finally find connection with other post-abortive women.

For my editor, Rebekah Benham, thank you for your time investment. You were prompt, reliable and skilled. And to Beth Cockerel, your attention to detail and the sensitivity and dedication with which you handled this vulnerable story, will never be forgotten.

To the employees and volunteers of Pregnancy Resource Services of Bremerton, Washington, thank you for your daily tireless work to provide resources, love, and support to expecting mothers, mothers of small children, and those needing resources for abortion healing. The volunteers of pregnancy resource centers do the hard work every day.

For my parents who have provided unwavering support and have walked with me for the last twenty years, witnessing first-hand how the loss of my son, their grandson forever changed me. Thank you for loving me, perfect mess and all.

To my stepdaughter—you have brought light and love into my heart, and I thank you for your unconditional acceptance of my story.

For my beautiful daughter, Lily (name withheld), may you one day fully know how much loving you was my greatest gift, and taught me how to love myself. You inspire me daily with your work ethic, strength, and maturity, and I'm honored to call you not only my daughter, but my friend.

To my husband, I give my love, respect and appreciation. While I drown you with words, I know I was living in a desert, yet you still loved me. Your patience and your grace in letting me love my son the way I need to, testify to the goodness and godliness of your heart.

RESOURCES

Deeper Still – Freeing the abortion wounded heart
Weekend abortion healing retreats and support
www.godeeperstill.org

The Silent No More Awareness Campaign
Education and awareness for abortion healing
www.silentnomoreawareness.org

Heartbeat International
Pregnancy help, outreach, and pro-life awareness
https://www.heartbeatinternational.org/

CareNet
National pregnancy center network and support services
Helpline: (877) 791-5475
www.care-net.org

Life Matters Worldwide
Partnership and resources for pregnancy care centers
www.lifemattersww.org

PATH: Post Abortion Transformation and Healing

https://www.facebook.com/groups/postabortiontransformationhealing

Rachel's Vineyard

Abortion healing retreat weekends

https://www.rachelsvineyard.org/

Isaiah's Promise

Support for families carrying to term after a severe or fatal prenatal diagnosis

https://isaiahspromise.net/

Perinatal Hospice Directory

Perinatal hospice and palliative care programs and support

https://www.perinatalhospice.org/list-of-programs

Support After Abortion

Abortion healing worldwide

www.supportafterabortion.com

Men and Abortion Network

Emotional healing resources for men who have lost a child to abortion

https://www.menandabortion.net/

Abortion Changes You

Abortion healing resources

www.abortionchangesyou.com

Hope After Abortion

Abortion healing resources

www.hopeafterabortion.com

SaveOne

Helping men, women, and families recover after an abortion

https://saveone.org/

Ramah International

Finding spiritual & emotional peace

https://ramahinternational.org/

APPENDIX B:

RECOMMENDED READING

Healing the Hurt that Won't Heal by Karen A. Ellison
(High Bridge Books, 2019)

Surrendering the Secret by Pat Layton
(Lifeway Press, 2008, 2019)

Her Choice to Heal by Sydna Massé
(David C. Cook, 2009)

For the Love of Angela by Nancy Mayer-Whittington
(Saint Catherine of Siena Press, 2007)

Worthy of Love by Shadia Hrichi
(Beautiful Voice Ministries, 2014)

Cradle My Heart by Kim Ketola
(Kregal Publications, 2012)

Forbidden Grief by Theresa Burke
(Acorn Books, 2002, 2007)

Forgiven and Set Free by Linda Cochrane
(Baker Books, 2015)

The Body Keeps the Score by Bessel van der Kolk, M.D.
(Penguin Books, 2015)

ENDNOTES

1. https://www.webmd.com/vitamins/ai/ingredientmono-542/laminaria

2. https://www.ncbi.nlm.nih.gov/pmc/articles/PMC2841012/

3. https://www.emdr.com/what-is-emdr/

4. https://www.cdc.gov/ncbddd/stillbirth/facts.html

5. https://www.marchofdimes.org/complications/miscarriage.aspx#:~:text=For%20women%20who%20know%20they,1%20to%205%20percent)%20pregnancies

6. https://www.cdc.gov/reproductivehealth/data_stats/abortion.htm

7. https://www.guttmacher.org/news-release/2017/abortion-common-experience-us-women-despite-dramatic-declines-rates

8. https://www.congress.gov/bill/108-congress/senate-bill/3

9. https://onlinelibrary.wiley.com/doi/full/10.7863/ultra.33.2.337

10. https://www.perinatalhospice.org/faqs

11. https://en.wikipedia.org/wiki/Onion

12. https://www.loc.gov/everyday-mysteries/food-and-nutrition/item/why-does-chopping-an-onion-make-you-cry/

13. https://medium.com/micrograph-stories

14. https://www.hypermobility.org/hormones-and-hypermobility

15. https://pubmed.ncbi.nlm.nih.gov/8646222/

16. https://www.psychologytoday.com/us/blog/all-is-well/201402/twins-and-cancer-nature-nurture-or-something-else

17. https://www.acog.org/clinical/clinical-guidance/practice-bulletin/articles/2013/06/second-trimester-abortion

18. https://www.psychologytoday.com/us/blog/media-spotlight/201302/when-parent-loses-child

19. https://www.massagetoday.com/articles/13825/Releasing-Emotions-Trapped-in-the-Tissues

20. https://www.psychologytoday.com/us/therapy-types/somatic-therapy

21. https://www.livescience.com/336-remember-traumatic-events.html

22. https://www.everydayhealth.com/fibromyalgia/101/what-causes-fibromyalgia.aspx#:~:text=%22The%20%5Bcurrent%5D%20consensus%20is,Joint%20Diseases%20in%20New%20York

23. https://www.webmd.com/rheumatoid-arthritis/ra-and-fibromyalgia#1

24. http://www.brainblogger.com/2015/01/24/how-does-post-traumatic-stress-disorder-change-the-brain/

25. https://www.scientificamerican.com/article/women-feel-pain-more-intensely/

26. https://www.psychologytoday.com/us/blog/somatic-psychology/201010/post-abortion-stress-syndrome-pass-does-it-exist